INTO THE HEART OF THE FEMININE

Also by Massimilla Harris, Ph.D. and Bud Harris, Ph.D.

Like Gold Through Fire: Understanding the Transforming Power of Suffering

The Art of Love: The Craft of Relationships: A Practical Guide for Creating the Loving Relationships We Want

Books by Bud Harris, Ph.D.

Cracking Open: A Memoir of Struggling, Passages, and Transformations

Sacred Selfishness: A Guide to Living a Life of Substance

The Father Quest: Rediscovering an Elemental Force

Resurrecting the Unicorn: Masculinity in the 21st Century

The Fire and the Rose: The Wedding of Spirituality and Sexuality

Knowing the Questions Living the Answers: A Jungian Guide Through the Paradoxes of Peace, Conflict and Love that Mark a Lifetime

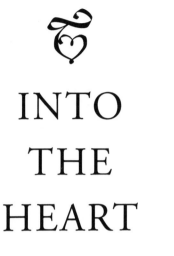

INTO
THE
HEART
OF
THE
FEMININE

Facing the Death Mother Archetype to
Reclaim Love, Strength, and Vitality

MASSIMILLA HARRIS, PH.D.
BUD HARRIS, PH.D.

DAPHNE PUBLICATIONS • ASHEVILLE, NORTH CAROLINA

Harris, Massimilla
Harris, Clifton T. Bud
Into the heart of the feminine: facing the death mother archetype to reclaim love, strength, and vitality / Massimilla and Bud Harris
Includes bibliographical references and index.

ISBN 978-0-692-31144-8   Non-Fiction
1. Psychology 2. Jungian psychology 3. Feminism 4. Spirituality 5. Mythology

Book Layout by Susan Yost
Cover Art & Design by Courtney Tiberio

Into the Heart of the Feminine Chapter-by-Chapter Study Guide PDF
Available for free at: http://budharris.com/books-2/into-the-heart-of-the-feminine/

Contents

Foreword

During midlife, we spent a magical period of years in Zurich, Switzerland, concentrating on learning Jungian psychology, knowing ourselves, and transforming ourselves and our lives. We were both there because in very different ways, our lives were no longer working and were not carrying us into a future that we wanted to live. In the midst of many days of tears, we had never felt more alive. We discovered that our inner worlds are vibrant, modern, and thriving. For the first time in our lives, we began to learn what it means to live from the feminine principle, to give time and attention to healing ourselves in order to allow ourselves to grow beyond our former limits. This book and our collaboration began there, and we hope that the book reflects the great love of life that Jungian psychology has opened in us. We have suffered a lot in our lives and lost too much to be completely at peace in a shallow sense, but we have gained a deep respect for life and affection for the human spirit. We are very different and independent people, but we love to collaborate with each other creatively. The voice of this book is the voice of that collaboration.

However, for the sake of clarity, we will use Massimilla's voice for the voice of the narrator in the book, because she will be sharing many of her personal experiences. Where it is appropriate, she will say "Bud and I." The pronoun *we* either will refer to Massimilla and a person she is working with or will be used in the collective sense.

The two of us have spent many evenings discussing the wounding of the feminine archetype and how it has affected us on a personal and cultural level. Bud and I believe this is one of the most urgent and important psychological challenges facing women and men today. The way our society has undermined and devalued this great archetypal force creates space for the deadly influence of the Death Mother, another archetype that entraps us and paralyzes our initiative, spirit, creativity, and vitality.

Our purpose in writing this book is to journey deep into the human and psychological dimensions of the wound to the feminine principle or archetype in our lives. We will call this wound the Death Mother archetype or complex. The power of the Death Mother, its negative force in our society, affects our culture in general, mothering in particular, and our ability to like, nourish, and take loving care of ourselves. The Death Mother has a devastating influence on a mother's ability to meet the emotional needs of a child. And many of us are held captive by the internalized effects of the wounded mothering we experienced as children. The healing path that will emerge as we proceed is based on the classic myth of Medusa, enriched with personal experiences and psychological insights that direct us toward healing and renewed personal consciousness. This journey will help us examine our assumptions about ourselves and our lives, in order to move from stagnation, inhibition, and even paralysis to full vitality, creativity, and—most of all—a deeper love of ourselves, others, and life.

The dreams and case histories that we share are intended for illustrative purposes. Except for our own stories and dreams, we have fictionalized and, at times, made composites of many case experiences. Our illustrations picture real life but are not connected to any actual individual.

This is a very special book for us. It began in Zurich when our lives transformed. Our debt to Jung and our teachers there is profound. The whole of our thirty-year journey has also been lovingly and courageously informed by Marion Woodman's work. Facing this wound, which has become virulent and which we describe as the Death Mother, is not really about death, but about life.

Introduction

I was born in Italy in 1949 into a patriarchal society. While I was in adolescence, it was taken for granted that my two sisters and I would go to work immediately after high school and bring our wages home to help pay for my two brothers to attend the university and finish their doctoral degrees. My father knew that I was intelligent, and he sent me to a business and secretarial school to ensure that I could get a good job. My sisters were also bright, but our parents and our culture expected us to fulfill our roles by getting married, having children, and making a home for our husbands and families.

By the 1960s, the cultural picture for women in the Western world was beginning to change. Meanwhile, I was still following the old path, working and bringing my money home until I eventually got married. By the time I reached my mid-twenties, the world of women was changing quickly. I was one of the first women to get divorced under Italy's new law legalizing divorce. Within a few years, I was pursuing my own doctoral degree in psychology while working and paying my own way through school. For my dissertation, I originated one of the first Italian studies of the new divorce law's effects on women. A few years later, I moved to Zurich, Switzerland, totally on my own, to study at the C. G. Jung Institute in order to become a Jungian psychoanalyst. While I was studying there, I met Bud, who was also studying at the Jung Institute. We were married in 1988 and moved to the United States in 1989.

There is no doubt that feminism and the changes it has ushered into our culture have opened many new paths and vistas for me and for other women. Yet I have become aware, both through my own growth and through the women who come to see me professionally and attend my lectures, that women and men in our society are still affected by an even deeper problem than inequality—though I value the goal of equality dearly. Many of the women that I have encountered are confused, depressed, and deeply disappointed in life. Most of them had achieved a so-called good life. Frequently, this good life contained a marriage, a career, and financial security that were now seeming to fall apart.

As self-awareness begins to dawn for many of us, we, both men and women, have discovered that our expectations have let us down. And in spite of a new age for women, we are still seeking to be comfortable within ourselves, to be confident in our own voice and values, and to be loved and understood on a personal level. At the same time, by midlife men are joining women in feeling trapped in their lives, frustrated, diminished, and untrue to their deepest selves. When people become parents, they face the added stresses of fear for their children's futures, financial commitments, a frantic busyness of activities, and, often, the heart-rending tensions of split families, single parenting, and joint custody.

Our lives are forced into busyness through children's activities, economic insecurities, job insecurities, relationship struggles, and our fear-inducing media images. Bud and I believe the pressures we are all experiencing in our lives have only added to the depression that affects so many people in our society. This depression has left us suffering to the extent that tens of thousands of us turn to food and medications because we are unable to find the true source of our unhappiness.

As the women's movement unfolded, we began to see one layer after another of women's suffering. The Jungian analyst Marion Woodman has spent her lifetime studying the feminine and has brought us to the heart of women's suffering in her discussions of the Death Mother archetype. In this book, Bud and I want to use our personal and professional experiences to expand and develop this work in a manner that makes it accessible to everyone. We believe doing this work can bring freedom, strength, and transformation in ways that can mean so much to all of us.

Feminism began to empower women in a fashion that had been needed for centuries. We all need equal opportunities, respect, fairness, and a chance for a fulfilled life in the world. The struggle to achieve these ideals remains, particularly for lower-wage earners, and this quest continues to be important. However, we must realize that seeking equality, respect, opportunities, and so on in and from the perspective of a patriarchal worldview creates a very one-sided approach to life.

Many of my female analysands painfully confess that they no longer have an idea of what it is to be feminine. Over twenty-five years ago, the Jungian analyst June Singer, in an article titled "The Sadness of the Successful Woman," said that she believed that such women are suffering from a particular form of depression: They are mourning for their lost femininity. She also considered this an archetypal problem because it affects all of us—women, men, and children. Singer points out that our patriarchal society places its highest value on the archetype of personal identity. The emphasis on fame in our culture epitomizes this idea. From preschool, to sports, to jobs, to careers, to where and how we live, identity in our culture is based on personal achievements. The terror that goes hand-in-hand with our idolatry of identity grips us when we do not achieve what we want to, plan to, or should accomplish. We must then face the shame of failure, of not being good enough, or of not being who we thought we were. No wonder losing a job, getting divorced, becoming seriously ill, or—even on a smaller scale—having our kid's team lose a game can fill us (or our kids) with shame. Shame haunts the identity-oriented person.

Singer has accurately suggested that matriarchal cultures are more relationship-oriented. Let me try to summarize her most important points. In a matriarchal society, our relationship to the group is the dominant value. Instead of being taught to succeed, children are taught to think of others first, to cooperate, and to subordinate personal goals to the general welfare. Guilt becomes the haunting terror in this type of social structure: the guilt of not living up to the expectations of others and of internalizing feelings that we are not living up to our obligations. Too often conformity seems to offer safety in this type of social-value system.

We see a different picture if we look at our patriarchal culture. In it, we sacrifice relationship values in order to fuel our quest for success in identity achievements. We make these sacrifices so frequently that we have lost the capacity not only to ground our relationship values in life but even to be aware of what our relationship values are. In the long run, we must learn that our personal identity is most satisfying in the context of relationships and is enhanced by our ability to love and appreciate the uniqueness and value in each other.

Still, the meaning of being feminine—the universal meaning of the feminine archetype or the feminine principle in life—although it includes relatedness, is actually much broader and life-giving. Our society has been so one-sided that it has limited the true meaning of the patriarchal to identity and achievement and has reduced what Singer calls the matriarchal and the broader feminine principle to an inferior function in our collective psyches. This relegation devalues the feminine principle's potential to guide how we live and represses it into our unconscious, putting it out of reach in our everyday lives. And here is where the situation gets more complicated and darker: *When the feminine principle is repressed into our unconscious, it becomes part of our collective shadow, and this shadow projects itself as a longing, or even a demand, for power.* In feminism's early days, activists projected the idea that men had the freedom that women wanted, and this projection, of course, carried a lot of anger toward men. But these kinds of projections, even projections such as "God the Mother," leave us in the predicament of trying to actualize the feminine by approaching it through the old patriarchal mode that dominates our society, including all of our institutions, no matter how much power they give to women.

Now, let's go back to what Marion Woodman challenges us to do. She calls us to go beyond the one-sided model our society is stuck in, to go beyond the incomplete model of the matriarchal as relational, and to undergo a long, deep, soul-searching, and demanding journey into our unconscious, into the world of the wounded feminine principle— into the world of the "Death Mother" as the personification of that wound. That is our goal as we travel through the pages of this book. Our purpose is to take this journey into healing the feminine, healing ourselves, healing women and men alike, and healing our culture to transform the very core of how we experience life.

You can see that my early experiences have led me deep into the challenges of finding and creating my own identity and deciding how to relate to life, myself, and others. As the early pages of this book will show, I have discovered that the Death Mother was a hidden theme behind the other themes in my life and work. With maturity, I can see that I was born into the necessity to do this work, and I have been wrestling with it, as Bud has in his own way, for as far back as I can remember. I know that we as women in the United States are better off in many ways than ever before. I am even more grateful when I compare my life to the lives of women around the world. But a destiny has compelled me to transcend the values of my culture, to pursue schooling beyond my conventional education, to travel to Zurich, and to make a life's work out of the quest for healing and wholeness. Now Bud and I are compelled to go further into this wound—this wound that is powerful, that exerts a force in the culture that shapes all of our lives—and try to discover the treasures hidden in healing and transforming it.

The obvious question is, how can we go into the long, deep, soul-searching journey of understanding the Death Mother? *Understanding her as the primary symbol and force of the wounded feminine principle in our lives will help us heal and transform ourselves in the process.* Then we will have released ourselves from the pressure of a disturbing tension in our lives and opened the doors to inner warmth and security. We will also have created the foundation for a strong, unique personality that can live in warm, loving relationships.

The Death Mother archetype, which we will define more fully later, is of course the opposite of what we think of as the good or nurturing mother. Our real mothers always leave us with a promise that can't be fulfilled because they can never fully match the good archetypal mother image that is inherent in our psyche. But our mothers are our first contact with the world of the feminine and the world of our emotions, which are closely related. Emotions are part of our biology. Emotions are powerful, vital, highly significant forces that can threaten us, reveal problems, paralyze us, and turn us into stone. They can also lift us up, animate us, and pull us into love and ecstasy. They are the means by which we engage in and measure our engagement in life. Our emotional life begins with our mothers, and the emotional power of the Death Mother today lives in the background of our lives while our pursuit of identity dominates the foreground.

In one of her classic interviews (*Spring*, Vol. 81) Marion Woodman writes that "the Death Mother wields a cold, fierce, violent and corrosive power. She is rampant in our society right now." The Death Mother is the name we give to a particular destructive force, a psychological complex operating in our personalities and in our society. It is a metaphor that helps us understand the devastating influence of this psychological complex, which saps the life, spirit, and resilience of many women and men. It paralyzes us emotionally and drains the values and possibilities for love from our lives. Writing about healing and transforming this wound has led Bud and me to organize this book into four sections.

In Part 1, Facing the Death Mother, I will share more of my journey into this arena and the psychology of personal experience that we need to know. I will describe what it means to face an archetypal problem and what kinds of changes we can make in ourselves. In order to understand ourselves in relation to this powerful force, we must look into ourselves in a more profound way than we ordinarily do.

In Part 2, A Healing Path, we will look closely at the ancient Greek myth of Medusa as a metaphor that explains how the Death Mother developed as a part of who we are. As the myth unfolds, we will also discover how we can heal and transform this damaging energy in our lives, which can move us from a state of paralysis into living with full vitality and creativity.

In Part 3, Burning Clean, we will continue to explore the hidden contempt for the feminine in our culture, what the wounded feminine is, and how it shows up in the lives of us all—men, women, and children. A road map for seeing how the Death Mother affects our lives will evolve as we burn clean from our illusions and defenses.

Part 4, The Freedom to Come Home, helps us remember that creativity once begun has the potential to continue. Love has the same possibility if it is nourished. We are never lost if we can become creative and loving in our own right.

As we are freed to come home to ourselves, we discover that every act of creation adds to the creativity in the world. Every act of healing does so as well, and so does every act of love. As our journey concludes, we will see that the transformation of the Death Mother's influence within ourselves forces us to become as complete a person as we have the capacity to be. The process that includes healing and becoming as conscious as we can brings out our hidden talents and helps us realize our own innate knowledge.

Bud and I hope that you will join us in undertaking this journey with strength, hope, determination, and love.

PART ONE

Facing the Death Mother

Where love reigns, there is no will to power;
and where the will to power is paramount, love is lacking.
The one is but the shadow of the other…
an unconscious Eros always experiences itself as a will to power.

– C. G. JUNG

Chapter 1

FACING THE DEATH MOTHER: REMEMBRANCE OF THINGS LOST

I can't tell you the number of people—men and women—who have sat in my office sobbing, saying, "Nobody ever saw me. Nobody had time to listen. So I am unlovable"—the saddest word in the language…And they mean it. As a child, that person was raised where the feminine was not present. You have to experience the feminine to understand it.

– Marion Woodman

Love in our culture seems to wear many faces, and we have few objective ways to tell if we are really loved or not. If we consider our movies, our romance novels, the articles in our magazines, and even the tenor of our print and television advertisements, we may begin to wonder if love has become an inaccessible experience for most of us. Is it something we can only read about, watch on a screen, or dream about but never truly experience? One of the most unconscious and yet driven of our ongoing activities is the pursuit of feeling loved and secure. But too many of us have become battle scarred and have pulled away from even hoping for love. Both in our relationships with others and with ourselves, we often find love difficult to define, to trust, and to take comfort in.

Perhaps this difficulty isn't so hard to understand if we carefully consider (1) how we came into the world, (2) the central symbolism of the archetypal feminine's place in our world and lives, and (3) how our culture has wounded and displaced this basic foundation of life. When we first come into the world, we are small, fragile, and defenseless. We are totally dependent on the love and care of our parents, especially our mothers. In our modern society, we have learned very well how to take care of the physical, biological, and even the developmental needs of our babies, even though parents at various socio-economic levels still face vastly different challenges as they meet their infants' needs. But we have let a vital need, the one whose fulfillment will determine our ability to have a feeling of self-worth and security, slip through the cracks of modern life. If our emotional needs are not met at the right time, we will face a daunting task later in life as we try to heal the structural wounds of our personalities. Like a plant that doesn't get enough water or sun early on, we will have trouble growing to our full height, no matter how much fertilizer we get later. Fortunately, unlike plants, we can direct our consciousness and self-awareness toward healing, which can give us new foundations for fulfilling our lives.

As helpless babies, we needed as much of our mother's and father's love and attention as it was possible for them to give. Having this love and attention is more important in the first year than in the second, and in the second year than in the third. Although this need decreases somewhat with time, it remains present in the background of a child's life. The need for love and attention acts as both a stimulant and a supportive container for our developing psychological foundation. By the time we are old enough to form permanent memories of childhood, the major events that shaped us—good and bad—have already happened. For those of us who had a rough time in these early years, denial—the failure to remember them—may be an unconscious emotional solace. A few of us may have experienced events so traumatic that they are seared into the memory cells in our bodies; we remember events that are beyond the possibility of most people to remember from such early years. For better or for worse, the way we are, the way we speak, the way we think of ourselves and others, our ease or fear about being in the world, our capacities for self-confidence, and our ability to give love despite early wounds and unsatisfied needs are evidence of our early experiences.

4

Trust Versus Mistrust

The image of the mother cradling her infant is a symbol of the state of inner harmony that seems as old as our history. The foundation of our emotional and psychological relationship to life rests on our personal experience of this metaphor as infants. According to the psychoanalyst Erik Erikson, who made a life's work of studying childhood and identity, we carry into adulthood a basic attitude of trust or mistrust in life, and we form this attitude as a result of our experience of early bonding.

A basic mistrust of the world, of life, and of our abilities to function competently in life affects us in many ways. Bud and I have seen many instances of these effects in our work with analysands. John, for example, was a tall, intelligent, and likeable man. Married with two children, he was also a busy, successful businessman who realized in analysis that his basic achievement was based on an underlying fear that at some point his world was going to fall apart. Andrea, another woman in our practice who was finishing college after raising two children and working in various retail stores, was a hardworking woman who realized that she had been depressed all her life. Well into his forties, Steve was a man who expanded the business left by his father and was now a self-made millionaire. But he was continuing to have dreams of being on his old college campus, unable to find the right room in which to take his exams. John, Andrea, and Steve are all trapped in a basic fear or mistrust of life. Many people with this attitude believe that if they let themselves get truly angry, their rage will destroy the people they love. If they even think about letting their caged animal of rage out, they unconsciously fear they will be destroyed by the people close to them. Others are trapped between their longings for love and the fear that compels them to live dishonestly and rigidly and to avoid intimate emotional depth with people close to them.

Now, let us consider some additional examples. When Marcia, who was the oldest of three children and whose mother had been a successful politician, was talking about what she wanted from her husband, she described it as being totally loved, supported, and accepted. She wanted to always be able to depend on his encouragement and his even

5

temperament. A few months into her inner journey, we came back to these ideas. I asked her how she felt about them now. She said, "You know, it sounds like I'm describing what I wanted from my mother. I'm not sure that can be a man's role." In another case I remember, Fred claimed that his girlfriend declared again and again that she loved him more than anything on earth and couldn't live without him. When I asked him how he felt about her comments, he replied, "This feels like I'm being eaten alive by her, and I am such a pleaser, so laid back, that I can't confront her demands."

These are a few of the struggles we face when we didn't get the love, attention, and security we needed in the years we were tiny. John was driven to achieve. Andrea was depressed. Steve's dreams showed an underlying sense of anxiety. Marcia searched for her "mothering" from her husband. And Fred could not stand for his own identity in his relationship. Others feared their anger, and most of these people also had a feeling of scarcity—there would never be enough understanding, love, and support in their lives. And deep down in their psyches was a dark pool of fear.

Do We Come Into Light or Darkness?

Parenting is undoubtedly one of the most challenging and misunderstood issues of our time. As babies, we embody the fundamental emotion, "I need you, and you need me." All people share this vulnerability—the fragile nature of existence and the sensitivity that is deeply human in parents as well as in their infant children. This equation, "I need you, and you need me" is basic. But it is neither obvious, fully conscious, or fully honored in today's world. The Italian language has a couple of verbs for saying, "A baby is born." They translate as "to come into the light." The literal meaning is "to come out of the darkness of the womb." But what if the baby is coming out of the darkness of the womb and into the symbolic darkness of a bleak, disturbed personal environment or the darkness of a culture that is unaware of the true needs of mothers and infants?

Parenting is not a natural instinct. Like all instinctual energies that call for action in life, parenting needs archetypal images to guide it. The archetypal image of the mother nursing the child that I mentioned earlier is such an image. But we live in an unnatural, diverse, and complex world, and we need to know more specifically what good mothering looks like and what bad mothering looks like. We suffer from a similar lack of archetypal images of fathers. We all know that neglect, abuse, sarcasm, and shaming are bad parenting. To complicate matters even more in the world of parenting, our sins of omission can be as bad as or worse than our sins of commission.

Let us consider an interesting example from recent history. Think about people born in the 1930s and 1940s, who became teenagers in the 1950s. The parents during that era endured the great stresses of the Depression and World War II, which of course were detrimental to good parenting. To make matters worse, a prevalent approach to care of infants at the time was so-called scientific child rearing. In other words, babies were put on rigid schedules of feeding and sleeping. Authority figures often suggested letting babies cry until they adjusted to the schedules. Can you imagine what this withholding of touching, nurturing, and feeding did to the basic bonding mechanism between mother and child? Should anyone be surprised that by the time these children reached their early teens, almost all of them felt compelled to "go steady"? A compensatory compulsion to fill an unmet need for early bonding, going steady rarely led to successful adult relationships. The need for bonding also led to a number of failed marriages because marriage can't really fill mother-child needs. Bud and I find it surprising that this cultural phenomenon, which didn't seem to exist in previous or following generations, has yet to be widely studied.

Bud and I experienced all of these wounds. Jung was quick to say, "Physician, heal thyself," and this must be the basis of our work. So, in writing this book we have revisited the depths of our own wounds and gained a new understanding of Jungian psychology's capacity to help us understand them, see how they are connected to our culture, and heal them. The following dreams reflect my feelings upon entering this work.

Challenge and Complexity

I would like to share a dream that I had while I was developing my lecture about the Death Mother. As the dream ended, I awakened in fear and awe, shaken to my core and at the same time inspired. I had dreamed that in my hands, I had a large piece of glass of some shape, thin and crunchy, but it was broken into pieces large and small. I started eating it, as if that were a normal thing to do, and I wondered if it would destroy my stomach. But before I could think about this further, I had finished the last piece. Then very slowly, I pulled a beautiful chandelier from my mouth, as if in some way I were giving birth to it. It came out unbroken, beautiful, and full of light.

This dream reminded me of Catherine, the heroine in Emily Brontë's passionate classic, *Wuthering Heights*, who said, "I've dreamed in my life dreams that have stayed with me ever after, changed my ideas; they've gone through and through me like wine through water, and altered the color of my mind." This was one of those dreams for me. At the time I was working on my lecture, I felt the material was too hard, the memories too painful, and I feared the whole project might overwhelm me. But this dream encouraged me to face this task and carry it through. It showed me that I needed to take in the reality of what I was experiencing, personally and professionally, as I worked on understanding the Death Mother and the depth of the wounds to the feminine in myself, in other people, and in our culture. The dream helped me face this project even though it was difficult, demanding, and even dangerous. It also showed me that as I worked through these issues, my psyche would metabolize them and bring them out greatly transformed, in a manner that would give us light. This dream became the guiding star that led Bud and me through the darkness of this work, which included some of the most difficult and painful memories, wounds, and self-confrontations in my life.

As we go through this book, it will be important for us to remember that as we face life, we encounter it with two voices. It is a cliché to say "from the head and from the heart," but we must be familiar with the importance of rational thinking in our world and also connected with our very human voices of love, meaning, and values. When this dream came, I was struggling to give voice and form to painful experiences that shaped me, that I encounter daily in my professional work, and that act in our culture in ways that affect not only us but also our children and grandchildren. I also remembered that many of the greatest scientific achievements have not been based simply on hard critical or even brilliant thought processes, but on dreams and imagination. Our imagination is the place where our conscious personalities and the many parts of our unconscious can meet each other, struggle, play, dream, and transform us. Initially, our imagination is where we must seek to confront, heal, and transform the Death Mother within ourselves.

The Feminine Principle: The Foundation of Life

When we begin to talk about the feminine principle, it is very hard to separate it from our ideas of gender and from the wounds we have all received in our struggles for recognition, empowerment, respect, and equality. This differentiation is so difficult because the feminine principle, as an archetypal part of all of us, also transcends our identities, and yet many of its characteristics are not only discounted but actually ruthlessly denied in our culture. I will give more details about this in a later chapter. When it's all said and done, our concept of the feminine principle as one of the two great archetypal foundations in life— whether you call them masculine and feminine, creative and receptive, or yin and yang—is most often associated with the Great Mother. One of the most common images associated with the archetype of the feminine is the Venus of Willendorf, which is clearly a mother figure. It is a statuette of a female figure with large breasts and a large belly. It was found in the village of Willendorf, Austria, and the statue's origins date back to between 28,000 and 25,000 BCE. Over the centuries, of course, many other archetypal figures of the feminine have evolved as various pantheons of goddesses that all represent aspects of human nature. But the Great Mother remains a primary one. In his book *The*

Great Mother: An Analysis of the Archetype, the Jungian analyst Erich Neumann explains that the Great Mother has two essential positive characteristics. The first he calls elementary, and its positive attributes are to nourish and protect, to give warmth and security. The second characteristic he calls transformative, and the accent here is on the dynamic element of nature, which has an inherent urge toward motion and change, growth and transformation. Of course these two characteristics have their negative counterparts as well, which can become devouring and destructive. Neumann calls these negative characteristics the Terrible Mother.

Most of us are familiar with these patterns. From these images, we have taken the step of considering Mother Nature the source or womb of all life. Nature is bountiful, often seeming to give continually without limits. But nature can also be ruthless, killing and devouring without reservation. Because of this reality, humans throughout history have attempted to live with nature, conquer nature, or influence it through religious rituals. The situation with our own human nature is different. Through conscious awareness and our efforts to get to know our nature more thoroughly and to heal the wounds to it we have experienced, we can cultivate its positive characteristics. When we live in ways that thwart our nature's good intentions, we thwart her life-giving qualities, and they bury themselves deep in our unconscious and turn destructive.

Our attitudes toward our own nature begin with the first personification of nature, the first feminine figure, we encounter: our mother. For most of us, the first woman we experience is our mother. Her fundamental purpose in our life is to hold us; give us warmth, food, and nurturance; and to care for our bodies. Her power is extensive, and she can easily fill our tiny hearts with fear, feelings of helplessness, and even rage. But she can also fill our little worlds with comfort and security as she nurses us, rocks us to sleep in her arms, and tends to our emotional and physical needs. The relationship between a mother and a baby is one of nature's most beautiful mysteries and is shown in art and sculpture throughout the centuries. But as Neumann points out, just as nature can be cruel, so can mothers. The Terrible Mother can be destructive in many ways. In her devouring form, she may keep her children fixated in a nightmare of infantile dependence and through a smothering psychological attachment, often disguised as love, inhibit their development, using them to fulfill her own selfish desires and neurotic needs.

The devouring mother as an aspect of the Terrible Mother becomes the archetypal foundation of what we call a negative mother complex. As I will explain further in our discussion of complexes, this kind of negativity takes over our personality completely at times and shades its perspective all of the time. The negative mother complex becomes the lens through which we see the world and the way we expect life and other people to treat us, which frequently has nothing to do with the reality we are experiencing but cannot see because of the tinted lens we have.

Negative complexes arise from a variety of wounds and experiences. All complexes are combinations of at least three experiences we have. First, they are based on our own personal wounds and experiences of growing up. In addition, our parents and grandparents, through their psychology, pass on to us their wounds, unsolved problems, and unlived lives. Finally, the neuroses—the out-of-balance or one-sided aspects, the conflicts, and the inadequacies—in the social character of our culture affects our experiences as we struggle to form our identity and feel secure in the world. The Death Mother is the foundation of a destructive complex that is both personal and cultural, and it is a special form of the negative mother. With certain complexes, we cut off some of our particular gifts and are unable to live out some of our potentials. But the Death Mother causes us to cut off the essence of life within us.

A Look at the Negative Mother Complex

Let's look at several examples that can help us understand the difference between a negative mother complex and a Death Mother complex. I will use the stories of four people to illustrate my points, and I will refer to these people again in future chapters. Timothy was a successful attorney who had grown up in what he thought of as a normal family. His father had been an attorney and later a judge. While his mother had been a housewife, she had been more devoted to tennis and social causes, leaving her children with a housekeeper. Timothy had earned a substantial amount of money until the recession cut his income almost in half. Shortly before the recession, he and his wife had divorced, ending up with joint custody of his four children. He was unable to confront his wife over the amount of alimony he was paying her, which was based on his former income. During a joint session with his children, Timothy's oldest daughter said he had never been able to confront his wife. His daughter went on to say that she could never figure out what he wanted, except to make enough money to keep everyone happy. Of course, he was frustrated and depressed. While he was organized and aggressive in the courtroom, he was passive and disorganized in his personal life. At the heart of his problem is a negative mother complex that frustrated his ability to crystallize his own personal values and find the strength to live them.

Anton was a tall, rather introverted, middle-aged biology teacher in a community college. His third marriage had just ended, and he had two children from his first marriage. He despaired of ever being able to have a loving relationship and missed his children. Anton felt like he was a good guy. He was rarely angry and tried to keep everything harmonious around him. Like most people with a negative mother complex, his mother had been the more influential parent in his life. She had been very emotional, and her ambition was for him to become either a minister or a doctor. In response to her emotionality, he had learned to deny his feelings to the point that he had trouble knowing he had them at all. He just assumed that he wasn't upset, angry, or hurt until his depression caused him to seek help. His negative mother complex, buried deep in his unconscious, sapped his self-esteem because he had not lived up to her expectations. She also sapped his energy and his ability to experience his emotions and be engaged in life. His first few sessions of analysis revealed that he didn't have any idea what was happening to him. Such is the power a negative complex may have.

Erin, my third example, was an energetic, gifted pediatric nurse. In her mid-thirties she began experiencing a haunting dissatisfaction in her work. Unsure what to do, she came in for analysis. Early in our work, it became clear that she always went the extra mile in her work and her relationships. She said, "Of course, I've known for years I'm a perfectionist and a pleaser. But I've also been pretty active in taking charge of my life." The reality was that as was the case with Anton, Erin's mother had been the emotionally dominant parent and had been highly anxious herself. Erin learned early in her life that she had to make great efforts to have any hope of getting her needs recognized and met. She seemed to compensate for the basic fear of life that she had inherited from her mother by acting as if she wasn't afraid at all. But her negative mother complex had driven her to be a perfectionist and a pleaser until it was draining her of her ability to enjoy life.

A Look at a Death Mother Complex

In my fourth example, Margaret's story is a different one altogether. She was the daughter of an affluent southern family and now was in her mid-fifties. Her father was a surgeon and her mother a socially active woman devoted to a number of clubs as well as political and social causes. Margaret described the only warmth she received in childhood as coming from the family maid. The house was run like a model of propriety. Everything was nice. Every meal was planned. Supper was eaten daily from china and silver. Margaret and her brother and sister went to private schools and good colleges. From a certain perspective, her life looked ideal. But it wasn't. Her mother was cold and, if the truth were to be told, probably didn't like children, resenting them and envying Margaret's intelligence and opportunities. Margaret described her mother as the cliché of "the iron fist in the velvet glove." As Margaret grew out of childhood, her father spent more time away from home, at work and on fishing trips. During this same time, her mother became more stern and critical. Nothing seemed to bring her joy and happiness, and nothing ever seemed good enough. "By the time I was in college, I began to break down under the pressure to live up to her standards," Margaret related. "The school recommended that I see a psychiatrist, who put me on medication for a while. During a particularly low period, I became pregnant and had an abortion. From that point on, my mother considered me crazy and a failure, even though I graduated with honors and went on to graduate school."

Margaret summarized her situation after years of therapy by saying, "It was like I was taught I did not have the right to be happy, to have my own ideas, to love someone or expect them to love me back. In therapy, I realized I couldn't let myself really experience the wholehearted love of my own daughters, and I could not reach the deep feeling of love I knew I felt for them. The same was true with my husband. I realized that my mother had emotionally paralyzed my father as well as me. In some strange way, I even felt that if I had a moment of joy, I was betraying her. Yet I was caught in some hopeless, emotional cycle with her. I couldn't just tell her to go to hell and get out of my life. If I did, I felt like I would have no one, and I seemed to continue the hopeless path of trying to please her, make her see my caring for her, get her to acknowledge me or what? I don't really know. I just couldn't stop."

This cycle, which is now going on between three generations of women, is more than a negative mother complex. It reflects this family's experience of the Death Mother complex. There are many variations of this complex in other personal situations. But at a basic level, the complex reflects the wounds to the feminine in our culture. It reflects our devaluing of the elemental feminine, that is, the ability for us to hold, nurture, comfort, nourish, and value our own emotional and physical lives as well as those of our children and other people. The Death Mother complex also reflects our devaluing of the transforming aspects of the feminine, which include our ability to be patient, to be receptive to potentials, to bring forth new life in many forms, and to sustain the relationships these activities require.

❊ ❊ ❊

Let us take a look at a few of the attributes of the Death Mother complex, whether in a person or in our society.

She is:
Distant
Cold
Does not know me
Is not interested in me
Considers herself a victim
Doesn't have a heart for me
Thinks life is all about her
Is not appreciative
Is constantly judging
Is opinionated
Is full of negativity
Is cruel
Is abusive
Kills hope
Kills initiative
Kills creativity
Drains our energy
Wounds body, mind, and spirit

Looking at these attributes, we can see how different they are from those of the Good Mother or the elemental and transformative aspects of the Great Mother. In the next chapter, we will explore what complexes are, how we can spot them, and what they do to us. We must understand this aspect of psychology before we can begin to heal and transform ourselves.

Chapter 2

WHERE LOVE BEGINS

*There is no other closeness in human life like the closeness between a
mother and her baby—chronologically, physically and spiritually they are
just a few heartbeats away from being the same person.*

– Susan Cheever

I was very touched when I read, "From birth to death, love is not just
the focus of human experience but also the life force of the mind, de-
termining our moods, stabilizing our body rhythms, and changing the
structures of our brains…Love makes us who we are, and who we can
become." These are the words of the modern brain researchers Lewis,
Amini, and Lannon in their book on attachment theory and brain re-
search, *A General Theory of Love*.

Earlier I said that babies need all the love that we can give them.
I described being born into a loving situation as being born into "the
light." But what happens to us when we are not born into the light?
What happens when our mothers are not "good enough," and what does
that term mean? What happens when our mothers don't fully respond to
our needs? How does it affect us that in our culture, the feminine principle, or the archetype of the feminine, is so wounded that being "good
enough" is almost impossible? Let us keep in mind that an archetypal
wound means a basic wound to the very nature of who we are, personally
and collectively. In our society in general, and in many of us individually,
the most deadly influence of the negative mother is always present.

17

The author and Jungian analyst Marion Woodman has called the most extreme measure of the negative mother, the Death Mother. Archetypally, we image her as Medusa. Medusa's psychological energy, which is partially the result of the wound to the feminine in our society, is incredibly destructive because it initially comes to us from someone whose positive image and influence is fundamentally and vitally important to us at the beginning of our lives. This "someone" is the person we expect to love us and whose love lays the foundation for our capacity to love, to feel secure in life, and to trust its experiences. Far too often, we grow up trusting our mothers or trying our best to trust them, until we gradually come to the realization that our mothers weren't really there. They were absent, or they were anxious or dealing with their own turbulent, overwhelming lives. In other cases, we may slowly begin to realize that we were not welcomed into the world. We were not wanted, we were resented, or our mothers wished we were different—or even dead. Later in this book, we will see how the myth of Medusa can guide us in understanding how this wounding took place in our lives and how we can find healing for ourselves. But first, I will say a little bit more about what we mean when we refer to the "good enough" mother.

The Good Enough Mother

Today we live in a world where our children are scared. Our inner unity and security are split. Almost all of us are over-involved in the demands of our outer lives at the expense of our inner lives. Without realizing it, we have become so alienated from our own natures that we have practically forgotten they exist. Or we may be caught in a cycle of frustration because we realize we are split from our authentic selves but cannot figure out how to cultivate and nourish our relationship with ourselves. These problems started at the beginnings of our lives. Mother and child, as metaphor or concrete reality, are simply no longer safe in our world.

As I have already noted, early infancy is the time when the world of the family begins imprinting itself on our tiny psyches, and this is a critical time in our emotional development. We know by now that much of a baby's view of the world is filtered through the mother's body and the emotional attitudes her body reflects. Of course this means that the child of a mother who is overly anxious or is resentful of the birth will feel out of adjustment psychologically, and such feelings will be the beginning of a negative mother complex. When we grow up this way, our personality will be founded on a deep sense of anxiety, scarcity, and a mistrust of the world. In contrast, if our mother is sufficiently gentle, loving, and emotionally secure, she will help us develop a basic sense of trust in life and in our place in the world. This is the "good enough" mother described by D. W. Winnicott, the well-known child psychiatrist, in his book *The Maturational Processes and the Facilitating Environment*. Winnicott uses this term to counteract the false belief that mothers have to be perfect, a notion that provokes fear in many mothers. Winnicott also goes further to point out the important role of fathers in this process. The father's role, he says, is to provide the mother with the peace and security she needs to be a good enough mother.

Of course, my short explanation greatly oversimplifies this very important situation. We all know that life is complex, and the mother-infant relationship can be disturbed for any number of reasons, such as early deaths, illnesses, separations, or deprivations due to many different kinds of crises. My point here is that our familial fathers as well as the cultural fathers—what should be the real patriarchy—play an important role in fostering this important human relationship, the foundation of love in the lives of our children. In older times, the cultural fathers took responsibility for their roles. The positive side of the patriarchy should uphold life and security; protect women and children; and encourage health, education, and art. Today's patriarchy is a negative abstraction that has lost its character. Bud addresses these issues in his book *The Father Quest: Rediscovering an Elemental Force*.

Parents today face an additional responsibility: We all need to learn how to defend our families from fear. In a society where our identity, and therefore our self-worth, is based on achievements and accomplishments, anxiety—which is fear—accompanies us on a daily basis. This is often, as I said earlier, a fear of being shamed. Also, our culture's wounding and belittling of the feminine and its values has led many mothers to mistrust the world and men to a greater extent than ever before, and this mistrust inevitably becomes part of the emotional heritage of our children. To make things even more complicated, our media amplify terrible events to the extent that fear permeates the atmosphere that we live in every day. Further, we have created a society with an economic system that essentially requires both parents to work, almost guaranteeing stress for young parents and an overly demanding burden on single parents. Ultimately as human beings, our primary sense of security through life often comes from caring, trust, and emotional closeness, but our sense of family and our sense of community are also very strained. The threats to parenting in our world are more complicated and serious than ever. And here we come back to the positive mother: It is the role of the good enough mother to turn her full attention to bearing and nurturing her baby. Some cultures value this role more than others. For example, some European countries give a new mother nine months' leave from work after her baby is born, guaranteeing her the same salary and job seniority on her return to work. It is the role of a good enough father to try his best to create a safe world and a protective covering for the mother and child—a protected covering "to bring forth the future."

Later, as our reflections continue, we will explore how the effects of the Death Mother, personally and socially, are operating to undermine the roles of the good enough mother and the good enough father and how we can transform this destructive force.

Our Own Truth Is Important

Learning how we are really wounded, how our childhood was lacking, and how we need to be healed and grow is crucially important to living a fulfilled life. If we aren't able to determine and face the truth of how we were formed, then in our radical achievement- and identity-oriented society we will constantly blame ourselves for what we consider to be our failures and inadequacies. Let me make it clear that blaming ourselves is not taking responsibility for ourselves. On the other hand, seeking the truth about ourselves and how we became who we are is taking responsibility for ourselves. Blaming ourselves usually means that we are on a constant search to find new ways to discipline ourselves and new programs to improve ourselves. When these efforts flounder, we risk creating a growing pool of deep inner shame, as we never seem to be able to come to who or what we want or are striving to be. If we consider the analogy of a house, we can see that remodeling or adding on to a structure is never really satisfying when there are preexisting problems in the foundation or the design of the structure.

At this point in our discussion, remembering we are in an identity-oriented society, we can easily understand why we find it difficult to develop a healing love for ourselves in order to compensate for the love that many of us missed early in our lives. Such a love, like the love from a good enough mother, would enable us to have the compassion needed to suffer with and accept our wounded parts and to deal with our failures and transgressions with mercy, kindness, and forgiveness. But here is our hurdle: Mercy, kindness, and forgiveness are qualities that the influence of the Death Mother in our world stops cold, particularly when these attitudes need to be directed toward ourselves.

We go on blaming ourselves—for not being loved; for early failures and missed opportunities; for choices we made in youthful ignorance or desperation; for abuse we experienced; for the distance, coldness, and angry attitudes of our parents; or for dishonest or cruel acts we suffered. Out of fear, shame, and confusion, we have bottled up these events, particularly the emotions around them, and buried them deep in our unconscious. All too often we expend so much energy to keep them there and protect ourselves from these emotions that we are unable to put much intensity into the rest of our lives. The flow of mercy, kindness, and forgiveness is blocked. The power of the emotions around these early traumas and our insistence on blaming ourselves or thinking we should be strong enough to overcome them will rob our spirit of its urge to grow and may stunt it completely. As we search for our own truth and begin the quest for loving ourselves, so that we can be our own good enough mother to ourselves, we need to keep in mind that birth comes out of darkness. And in the ancient tradition of the alchemists, darkness was a necessary condition for purification and transformation. The reality of the early events in our lives and their powerful emotions that we have tried to keep locked away in the dark, defensive compartments of our souls need to be brought into the light so we can begin refining them through our hearts until compassion can turn them into gold.

Examples of Personal Truth

Let's take a look at several of the people I mentioned before and see how they responded to my ideas about the good enough mother and father. It will be helpful to hear their comments as they realize the truth about their early realities. You may remember Timothy, the successful attorney who had grown up in what he considered to be a normal family and was unable to confront his former wife during their marriage and after it, when she was taking advantage of him financially. During our discussion, Timothy said that his mother had never been home when he was small because she was so heavily involved in clubs and charities, tennis and golf. When growing up, he always wondered if she liked him or liked children. The fact is he needed his mom. He was a little guy, small in stature, and was lonely and intimidated by preschool and kindergarten. He became compliant at an early age and tried desperately to earn any little crumb of attention or affection he could get. But he never got crumbs of affection from her. "She doesn't hug me or any of us to this day," he recalled in one session.

"But that is only the beginning," he continued, "As I listen to you talk about the negative mother, I realize that I learned from the start to try to ignore my needs for love, support, and affection. Damn! I learned to deny and block them, not ignore them. I learned to be a 'good boy' and I became less of a person in the process. I learned that what little acknowledgement I got came from getting good grades, achievement, and that seemed to be the only way I was valued. I was proud of my grades, but felt like they always had to be better and better. The pity is that now

22

I don't even know how to figure out what I need. No wonder my ex-wife used to say it seemed like nobody was at home inside of me."

Timothy was beginning to understand the reality of his childhood. As he came to understand his life better, he realized that there are no shortcuts to help him identify his needs or the feelings he has and had about them. He was shocked to discover how reluctant he was to ask for love and for help from the people closest to him. For now, like Timothy, we are learning to face our reality. Later in the book, we will see what to do next, once we have accepted it.

Andrea provides us with another corroborating example. She was hardworking and, as a single mom, was finishing college after raising her two children. During our work together, she gradually realized that at some level, she had been depressed all of her life. When we talked about her early years and good enough parents, her story unfolded. Andrea had been the oldest of three children. Her mother was an alcoholic and had a nervous breakdown after the birth of her third child. When Andrea was fourteen, her father lost his job, and the only new job he could get required him to travel. So, at fourteen, Andrea became responsible for the family most of the time. In addition to doing her schoolwork, she had to take care of her little brother and sister, the house, meals, laundry, and her mother. "I did what I had to do," she said, "I didn't even think about being loved. I never said 'no' because I couldn't see any alternatives. I just endured whatever was going on and hoped I would be able to take a breath when I grew up. I knew I was angry and depressed during high school because I knew everyone else had a life. When my despair and rage were too much to bear, I would cut myself to feel some release. Then I married the first man I could. I was so desperate to have a life. At first, he seemed like the first person who really saw me, listened to me, cared about how I felt, and at least for a moment, I thought I could trust him. He was wonderful when we dated, but he later turned out to have a drinking problem and got emotionally abusive. But I was so hungry for adoration, to be needed, that I endured him for years. Finally, I knew I had to get my kids into a better environment."

As we worked together, I was impressed by Andrea's ability to endure. What had once been a survival strategy and later trapped her in a bad marriage was now becoming the foundation for her work on herself. The effects of her parents on her were certainly damaging and wounded her deeply. Situations like these may seem exceptional, but I encounter these kinds of stories time and again. And I believe they reflect the profound influence of the Death Mother in our society. Looking at the great values of the feminine principle—relatedness, presence, an open heart, warmth, patience, and trust—I don't see these values being supported in our identity- and achievement-oriented society. They hardly exist in our worlds of work, education, and entertainment. They are also rare in our families and religious institutions. Bud and I can't begin to tell you how many people in our offices we've heard say, "Nobody tried to see me for who I really was," or "Nobody ever really listened to me," or "My parents were good parents, but I couldn't really go to them about anything I thought was serious." Then we might ask in response, "Whom can you trust today to give your truly heartfelt responses to? Can you truthfully trust to even give them to yourself?"

Erin is another person that I mentioned previously. Erin was a gifted pediatric nurse that began experiencing unhappiness in her work during her mid-thirties. She had commented earlier that she had always been a "perfectionist and a pleaser." I also noted that her mother had been the emotionally dominant parent in her life and was highly anxious. Even though she was approaching eighty years of age, Erin's mother continued to be a very dynamic and financially successful real estate broker. After a little reflection, Erin thought that her mother was driven to continuous work and success by her anxiety. Erin's father, who was now retired, had also worked, but in general he was quiet and passive and supported her mother. When we discussed the good enough mother and the wound to the feminine principle in our lives, Erin responded by saying, "Wow! I thought my mother was on the front line of feminism. She seemed to live out the refrain, 'I am woman. Hear me roar!' from her generation. But now I can see it is more than that. I believe she was also hurt, depressed, disappointed in her marriage, and bitter."

Erin paused, and I asked her to continue. "I never questioned much about what was expected of me," she said. "I had a few teenage moments. My mother was such a whirlwind, it was easier to just go along. Protesting was squashed anyway, and my father always took her side. Actually, I was rarely included in conversations. I can see how this whole process has carried over into my relationships. I am kind, forgiving, and accommodating by nature, or maybe by indoctrination, as I now see it. Yet I end up being angry at myself for not being conscious of when I'm being taken advantage of by family, friends, and even at work. Why have I been so angry at myself? Why have I wasted so much energy blaming myself, thinking that if I did things better or was more understanding, or not so needy, that my relationships would work out? I think it's time for me to start figuring out what my real needs are."

In many ways, Erin had built a good life for herself. So had her mother. She achieved the successful identity admired in our culture and longed for in her generation of women. Yet for Erin and her mother, something was missing. To go on with her inner work, Erin must pay careful attention to herself and take the time and space to be present to herself. She must recognize that important things have been going on inside of her for her whole life, things that need to be felt, said, grieved for, celebrated, and lived. She will then become stronger, love life more completely, and find herself grounded in authenticity. For Erin and for us, this inner journey depends upon uncovering and facing the truth of our own reality, the opening chapter of our story.

These are three brief, oversimplified examples. But they can give you an idea of how we can identify the needs we had in early life, examine what we experienced, and accept that for many of us, important needs went unmet. This acceptance provides the foundation for beginning the journey of healing and growth that will open the doors to the fullest promise our lives can offer. But before we go on, let's consider an example in which the influence of the Death Mother is as clear as crystal.

Facing a Deeper Truth

Deep beneath the systems of order in our organized lives, stormy forces are often at work. We see these forces in Margaret's story. Margaret came from a life that seemed ideal from an everyday perspective, and yet it became the example I would use of a woman's direct encounter with the Death Mother. Mythical kingdoms symbolize the deeper forces in our personalities—such as Inanna's tempestuous journey into the underworld or our glimpses into Greek mythology's underworld, with its passionate lord, Hades, and his bride, Persephone, who preside over the kingdom of the past and the ghosts of our ancestors. Fairy tales show us the stories of violent fathers, sick kings, absent queens, stepmothers, dwarfs, heroes, and magical creatures—all carrying on lives in our unconscious that parallel the daily lives of our conscious personalities. These little kingdoms of alternative consciousness, emotions, values, and ideas maintain their existence, often waiting for us to search them out and become aware of the tremendous power they may be wielding in our emotional processes, relationships, and the directions of our lives.

Jung developed an approach that lends clarity and organization to our study of the unconscious and the forces that move us. He described the foundation of these forces in his work on complexes, which we will investigate more deeply in the next chapter. He used myths and fairy tales to help us understand how these complexes are formed, how they act, and how they can be transformed and integrated in our inner work. We will consider the myth of Medusa as a guide to the process of transforming our experience of the Death Mother.

Frequently, we try as hard as we can to live in a "normal" state of maturity as defined by the conventional models of existence we learned from our families and society. Or we try to rebel against these models, seeking a more fulfilling way of life that we are unable to attain because we have not yet faced the reality that shaped us, hurt us, dominated us, and is still blocking our path, like an avalanche on a mountain trail. Let us return to the story of Margaret for a moment. When Margaret tried to live a conventional life or to rebel against the cold propriety and expectations of her mother, she ended up weeping and weeping, and the more she wept, the more furious she became at herself and at life. Something deep inside her was calling out for recognition and healing. As we recognize our painful inner voices, it will comfort us to

26

remember that the healing purpose of learning to understand ourselves in more profound, heartfelt ways isn't just to resolve our conflicts or to deal with our neuroses. Our deeper purpose is to join forces with the well of life and renewal within us. Individuation, as Jung called this process, connects us to the source of our evolving strength, wisdom, love, and other potentials. By embarking on this inner journey, we begin accepting our reality, healing ourselves, and opening the door to our true capacities for living.

Margaret was frightened and ashamed of her tendency to break down in tears in front of other people. She was shocked at the vehemence of the exclamations that poured out of her in my office. Choking back her tears, she said, "I just can't do it anymore. I can't get my life together. I yell at my children, my marriage stinks, and I don't know why my husband stays with me. I don't like him and I don't like myself. I hate the way I look. I hate looking crazy. I feel stupid, and the harder I try to...fix things, the worse it gets."

When Margaret stopped blaming only herself, she was able to begin explaining her anger with her parents. Previously, she had been directing her anger and fury inward, faulting herself for not being lovable and for not living up to their expectations. Yet Margaret had been unaware of how much she was blaming herself. She had resented her mother's relentless expectations, which always seemed to exceed anything Margaret could achieve. Margaret's experiences with her mother, her mother's coldness and disdain, had left her furious and had sabotaged her capacity to give and receive love. She was also devastated by her father's absence in general and his complicity with her mother when he was present. Bit by bit, Margaret began to realize that what looked like a childhood supplied with the "right stuff" was actually full of damaging events that had fashioned the plot of her life's story so far. As Margaret learned more about herself, she began to grudgingly respect her rage and despair as turning points that forced her to begin the efforts to open up her life, to heal, and to grow, rather than to give up.

When I began telling Margaret about the features of the good enough mother and how we could start to help her "mother" herself, I was surprised and confused by her initial response. She said, "I never thought that life could be full of so much heartbreak." When I asked her to say more about what she meant by her statement, she replied, "My little baby heart could never find the heart that it needed to enliven it. I never had a mom who could mother a child. My mother didn't even have a clue what mothering really means. I guess she never had her heart enlivened either."

As I waited quietly, she continued by saying, "There was never any true celebration of my life—that I was here. I always felt alone, on the verge of potential annihilation. There was never a safe preserve. No matter what I do, I will never be able to be loved by her, but her volatility and viciousness left me feeling worthless and like I could be abandoned at any moment. As I got older, I became more convinced that if I didn't live purely to please her, she would take pleasure in annihilating me. I simply hate her. I know she must have been terribly hurt herself, but I can't find any sympathy for her at all."

More than an ongoing negative mother complex, the painful cycle going on in this family for at least three generations reflects their experience of the Death Mother complex. There are many variations of this complex in other personal situations, but the feelings that emanate from it reflect the basic wounds to the archetypal feminine principle in our society. What I said previously bears repeating: The Death Mother complex reflects the basic wounds to the archetypal feminine in our personalities. It strikes a nasty blow to our ability to warmly hold, nurture, comfort, and nourish and to acknowledge the importance of our emotional and physical lives, within ourselves, with our children, and with other people. Further, the Death Mother complex reflects the devaluation of the transforming aspects of the feminine, which include our ability to be patient, to be receptive to new potentials and change, to bring forth new life in many forms, and to sustain the relationships with ourselves and with others that these activities require. We need to have the kinds of hearts that can enliven those in the new life we need to nourish, whether in our children or symbolically in the potential new being born within us.

Powers Beyond Our Control

It is worth mentioning here that as Bud and I were working on how to end this chapter, Bud dreamed that he was in an unknown place and was calling out, "Help! Help! Help!" In the dream, he knew that I would come and wake him up. This reminded us of Jung's statement in *Man and His Symbols*, p. 82, that "the one thing we refuse to admit is that we are dependent upon 'powers' that are beyond our control." He then goes on to say, "The motto 'Where there's a will, there's a way' is the superstition of modern man."

Jung continues in this way by writing, "Yet in order to sustain his creed, contemporary man pays the price in a remarkable lack of introspection. He is blind to the fact that, with all his rationality and efficiency, he is possessed by 'powers' that are beyond his control. His gods and demons have not disappeared at all; they have merely got new names. They keep him on the run with restlessness, vague apprehensions, psychological complications, an insatiable need for pills, alcohol, food—and above all, a large array of neuroses." As we drank our morning tea and reflected on Bud's feelings around the dream, we realized how right Jung was. We are dealing with more powerful forces than we like to realize. They are at the foundation of our lives and, to some extent, will determine how our lives unfold and how we will experience our futures.

I described some of the positive characteristics of the archetypal feminine principle in the opening chapter of this book. I use the word *archetypal* to emphasize that this principle is fundamental in our nature and that it is a power that is truly beyond our control. When we forget to honor and develop such a principle, we will pay a price. The energy surrounding this archetype will be pushed into our unconscious, as Medusa withdrew into her cave, and it will bring weakness, affliction, and disease into our psychological systems, which in this case will be both personal and collective. Jung considered the feminine principle to be one of relatedness that is necessary for us to be personally connected to one another and to life. Additionally, you may recall that Erich Neumann categorized this archetypal figure into two additional basic components. The first component he called elementary, and its positive attributes are to nourish and protect, to hold and contain, and to give warmth and security. The second attribute he called transformative. This aspect of the feminine principle is characterized by the dynamism found in nature, especially in our human nature, which has an inherent urge toward motion, change, growth, and transformation. We also looked at how these powers affect who we are and who we may become; when they have been wounded, they become negative in our psyches and experiences.

Before moving on, I would like to summarize a few more key points. In this chapter, we have explored the positive aspects of the feminine as the origin of love and security in our lives. We have seen how the positive aspects of the feminine come into life through our personal experiences of the good enough mother and how she is supported by the father and the culture. Of course, we don't have to realize these attributes perfectly in order to foster the development of our children or the new potentials seeking to be born and nurtured within ourselves.

We then looked at what happens when the feminine principle is wounded and our capacity to be good enough mothers is likewise wounded. The examples, though oversimplified, show the effects of these wounds through the personal responses of the people sharing them. Further, I believe they reflect experiences that most of us are familiar with, ranging from the examples of a negative mother complex in a man and in a woman to the example of the destructive power of the Death Mother complex. The balance of this book will address understanding, healing, and transforming these wounds. The efforts we put into this quest will free us from our past, strengthen us, and open us to a new future.

This work also brings to light the indisputable importance of the power of the Self, our true center and the image of the Divine within us. This treasure we carry within remains to some extent dormant, in the background of our lives, until we become conscious of it. The Self's inherent purpose is to bring us into the full expression and experience of our lives. Perhaps it is in this part of our nature that the potential for love really begins and then seeks expression through the feminine principle. One thing is clear: Knowing about the Self is a great source of hope for us. Listening to what the Self is trying to tell us assures us that life isn't about "getting it right." Of course, we want to do the best we can. But we must also remember the Self, this living force within us, wants to help us face our wounds and darkest moments and then—through hurt, fear, sorrow, anger, and tears—emerge and become healed and whole.

As we look further into how we can call on this part of ourselves for help, we will discover, as Jung did, that strong forces exist within us. Ultimately, the strongest one, the Self, is at the center of our soul. The seat of our inborn urge to heal and grow, the Self enables our personality, our life, and our story to become complete if we give our inner life the attentive, loving, supportive environment that it needs.

Chapter 3

TURNING POINTS

Eros, the function of humane feeling, intuition, and imagination, is empowered by love. Logos, associated with rectitude, is the rational function, master in the world of analytic thought…Jung says, "It is the function of Eros to unite what Logos has sundered."

– JUNE SINGER

When I came to the United States with my husband in 1988, I was filled with excitement and looking forward to my new life. Within a few short weeks, to my surprise, I was almost overwhelmed with a feeling of homesickness, "For what?" I asked myself. I realized that it was not my literal home or family that I missed so much. After all, I hadn't lived close to them for years. What I missed was the symbolic ground that had supported and contained my life. Not only my house, neighborhood, school friends, and acquaintances but an entire world of ideas, perspectives, and opinions that were familiar to me were at the roots of what I would call home.

Eventually we have to develop that ground within ourselves so that we can feel at home in ourselves and in our lives. In many ways on many levels, we long for home, search for it, and try to create it, or illusions of it, on holidays such as Thanksgiving, Christmas, and others. All too often our efforts leave us feeling vaguely empty or, worse, frustrated, lonely, and like failures. As I read Marion Woodman's works on the feminine, I realized that home, whether within ourselves or outside of ourselves, is a spiritual place, a place where the spirit of the arche-typal feminine is fully present and creates the ambience. No amount of food, presents, giant TVs, or other material things can create a home, either within us or in our lives, without the presence of the feminine spirit, the ambiance of the elemental feminine.

Marion Woodman's ideas about the feminine and, in particular, the Death Mother immediately made a lot of sense to me when I began reading them. A new understanding of myself and our culture began to come into focus for me. Later, I was just as surprised to see how many women and men were touched when I delivered a lecture titled "Facing the Death Mother: How to Move from Paralysis to Full Vitality and Creativity." Many people came from far away to hear my reflections on a topic that obviously struck a chord in them.

Initially, in spite of my feelings and intuition that the Death Mother is a force we all have to reckon with, I had to question myself, "Can I dare talk about this force? Is this force of the Death Mother alive in me, around me? Just as important, is she alive in the people I am working with?" I have known for most of my life that my mother was cold to all of her children, and moreover, she was envious of me. That envy grew with the years, as her efforts to put me down also grew. I knew that I came from a family that had been through its share of difficult times but whose social appearance was very good. Because my family's appearance was good, I initially wondered, "What's wrong with me?" As I came to realize the problem did not lie with me, I still had to ask myself whether my feelings about the power of the Death Mother were really true. And, in spite of the number of people who have responded to me, I still wondered, "Are these feelings true for most of us? Do most of us feel at some level like Harry Potter? Do we feel like we are in the wrong home, that these people who resent and diminish us aren't our real parents?"

In recent history, Harry Potter has been one of the most widely popular series of books around, among adults as well as children. As the series' first book, *Harry Potter and the Sorcerer's Stone*, opens, Harry is delivered to a home of people who were proud to say they were "perfectly normal, thank you very much." The family he was delivered to were "Muggles," people who, as we say in Jungian terms, sleepwalk through life and deny their own potentials for depth, wholeness, and communication with the more profound dimensions of themselves and life. Harry knew that Mr. and Mrs. Dursley would never understand him or value his potentials. They regarded his uniqueness with disdain and housed him in a closet under the stairs. It would be a long time before Harry would learn that he was special. Harry was taught, "Don't ask questions—that was the first rule for a quiet life with the Dursleys." The Dursleys often spoke about Harry "as though he wasn't there—or rather, as though he was something very nasty that couldn't understand them, like a slug." The home of the Dursleys could have been my home, or Margaret's. Margaret, as you may recall, came from an affluent family in which everything "looked good," but her parents were cold and distant, seeming to value social appearances above all else. This is a home dominated by the Death Mother, and our culture, too, is dominated by her.

In fact, when he was young, "Harry dreamed and dreamed of some unknown relation coming to take him away." In many ways I was like Harry when I was a small child. I was convinced that my mother could not be my biological mother. Many of us dream, wish, or hope that somewhere out there our "real" parents exist or that if we wait long enough and try hard enough, the parents we have will turn into real parents, "good enough" parents. Meanwhile, we live and grow up in a hidden world, often one of reading, filled with fantasies and magic. Like Harry's other world, the realm of our imagination protects us from being emotionally demolished. This world is our refuge until we develop the power to find or redeem our true parents, the archetypal positive mother and father within our own psyche. Like Harry found Hogwarts, we must find within ourselves a safe and nurturing place, the elemental feminine, or we will be in a never-ending losing conflict with the Muggles, the "normal" people who sleepwalk through life. I am convinced that these scenarios and what they touch in all of us are why these kinds of childhood books are immensely popular among both adults and children. They represent the secret feelings and longings in us. When such stories are really worthwhile, they use the words and images of our times to bring to life many of the timeless themes in fairy tales.

35

Harry Potter, Margaret, and I spent much of our early lives longing for the presence of the positive, nurturing feminine. Something deep inside of Harry, in the world of magic, knew he was special, and people meeting secretly in the depths of his unconscious were drinking a toast, "To Harry Potter—the boy who lived." That is the part of ourselves that we long to get in touch with—the part that finds joy in the fact that we are alive. This is the inner good enough mother, an important component of the archetypal feminine. The inner good enough mother values and respects us, sees and listens to us, and accepts that our thoughts, desires, and feelings are real and legitimate. Yet the wound to the archetypal feminine denies us all of these things. It is this wound and how we suffer from it without giving it the healing attention that it needs that fuel the fury of the Death Mother. An untended psychological wound becomes driven by its need for healing and transformation, a need that should now bring us to a turning point.

Awareness, Acceptance, Unity

Not too long ago, Bud and I spent some time being filmed walking through a labyrinth. In a few minutes, we were lost in the experience. The labyrinth was beautifully made of fieldstones, carefully arranged in natural settings. We couldn't see where we were actually headed. We simply had to follow the path, to trust we were on a path that would lead to a center. As we slowly walked, we began to feel more grounded, more centered, more contained in this experience of life. We also began to feel a sense of relief, freed from the "rationality and efficiency" that Jung said blinds us to everything else. We were being touched by the world of the archetypal feminine. As we are touched by the feminine and are able to step outside of our traps of rationality, efficiency, and "things that have to be done," we become more open to our innate wisdom. An awareness of our innate wisdom helps us understand the language of love, the mystical, art and poetry—the language of symbolism, metaphor, meaning, eternity, and, most of all, the real language of stories.

In his essay "The Symbolic Life," in volume 18 of his collected works, Jung writes that "only the symbolic life can express the needs of the soul—the daily needs of the soul, mind you! And because people have no such thing, they never step out of this mill—this awful, grinding, banal life, and therefore want sensation." Let us think about that statement for a moment. Could that have something to do with our constant blast of media and entertainment that is filled with conflict, sex, violence, and fear? Listen carefully to what Jung is saying, because he is explaining a very important key in understanding our lives. He continues, "These things go pretty deep and no wonder people get neurotic. Life is too rational, there is no symbolic existence in which I am something else, in which I am fulfilling my role, my role as one of the actors in the divine drama of life." Harry Potter must be outside the normal world of the Muggles to become a participant in the divine drama of life. The symbolic world and its languages are old friends of the heart, the soul, and, most of all, the feminine.

So far, I have talked a good bit about the opening in the story of Harry Potter. In olden times, we created culture by using stories to give a sense of form and meaning to our lives, to give us a sense of life's mysteries, and to connect us to these mysteries. Today we tell our children stories primarily to entertain them. They, in turn, hunger for the archetypal themes in stories that connect them to life and mysteries. But it is we, the adults, who are losing our abilities to understand these stories on a more profound level. The Harry Potter series is great entertainment. But what does its great popularity tell us about ourselves?

I have learned the most from our eminent wisdom traditions, our religions, by studying the stories that make them up and that they use to teach us. Like many people, I am also using Jungian psychology to help me re-imagine them in order to help them inform my life today. Many of us have also experienced the intimacy brought about by sharing our personal stories as we begin a new relationship. Throughout time, stories have connected us with each other, with our dearest values, with ways of living that give us meaning and healing, and with the divine and our deeper selves. A real story touches the mind, the heart, and the soul.

Unfortunately, though, we live in a world that is destructive to our experience of stories. Television gives us disconnected news blips, soap operas, sitcoms, and reality shows that have no deeper theme, while everything is fragmented by the insertion of commercials. Just as unfortunately, our movies that reflect archetypal themes and human dramas are couched in terms of entertainment, which robs these archetypal themes of their transformative power. Moreover, talk radio has no story to tell us and tries only to arouse our emotions—or as Jung might say, to bring sensations to banal lives. This public direction has caused us to develop a resistance to story in its more profound forms. The hum of noise, often referred to as white noise, placates our anxiety. The world supports our resistance to stories because to pay attention to them takes time and to reflect on them requires silence and listening.

Bud and I both began our Jungian experience by reading Jung's autobiography, *Memories, Dreams, Reflections*—his story. Every time I have reread this book (and I have done so many times), I am struck, in my own inner work and in my professional work, by Jung's assertion on page 117 that "the patient who comes to us has a story that is not told, and which as a rule no one knows of. To my mind, therapy only really begins after the investigation of that wholly personal story. It is the patient's secret, the rock against which he or she is shattered." And later on Jung says, "The problem is always the whole person, never the symptoms alone. We must ask questions which challenge the whole personality." In other words, symptoms arise from this blockage of our story, and we must discover the story of what is missing in our lives or what is affecting our lives in order to have our life become a story of authenticity, meaning, and fulfillment.

In the last chapter, I briefly shared some of the stories of Timothy, Andrea, Erin and, in a bit more detail, Margaret. From even these short vignettes, you can get some sense of their stories, the stories of their wounds and the stories of the major complexes affecting their lives. You may also get a general idea of the cover story they have been living.

Thinking about the quotations from Jung, you can see how important stories are. They represent the point of departure for "knowing" the people we are dealing with—their environment, their experiences, and their struggles. In Jungian psychology, when we try to understand a dream or a complex, we try to understand its plot and what it is like for us and for the characters in the dream to be in that particular story. So, as we look at dreams, we look at their classic structure. We reflect on the beginning scene, the opening place, the situation. Next, we analyze the complications, the flow of action or the lack of action, and any new complications that occur. Then we consider the climax of the action, the situation that is a turning point. Finally, we look at the result: what has been solved, pointed out, or left unsolved.

As we pay attention to and befriend our dreams, we are approaching them from the standpoint of a classic, dramatic structure. Seeing the dream as a story helps us understand its symbols. Let me share a simple example. Suppose as my dream opens, I am sitting in a car. I am sitting in the backseat, and my mother is driving. I might wonder how I am traveling through life and why my mother's effects on me are still in control, or I might ask what situation in my day has caused my mother complex to take over my life.

If we are willing to go through our dreams this way, one sentence at a time, we will be amplifying each dream into a broader story, and we will become more personally informed by their stories. When recalling a dream, it is useful to connect it with the story of our lives and see how the dream links us to that story. Dream stories that include figures that are the same sex as we are (in Jungian language, shadow figures) are telling us stories about our identities. Dreams with figures of the other sex (anima or animus figures) are telling us stories about our relationships to ourselves and others. Our dreams that feature archetypal images, ranging from our great myths to our great religions, speak to us about our destiny, transformation, deep healing, and other soul issues. And if we develop our dreams fully enough, we will usually discover a deeper theme or archetypal patterns.

In order to bring the feminine into our world, we must begin in a personal way. It is not an easy path, and we will quickly see how readily it conflicts with the patterns of our daily lives. But in order to value the feminine and have it become reborn within us, we must take the time to reconnect with the wholeness of who we are. We have to take the time to listen to our dreams, to write them down, and to reflect on our lives. Honoring the feminine means having the patience and taking the time, like Mary in the Gospel according to Luke, to ponder these things in our hearts. We must recognize that there are many things going on within us that need to be perceived, accepted, felt, said, lived, grieved, and raged over. We need to give these things our attention, concern, and understanding. In his writings, Jung explains to us repeatedly that nothing can be transformed until it is accepted. Acceptance, holding, and pondering in our hearts make up a basic part of our feminine nature, of the elemental feminine. In this process, we are also accepting that our inner life is valid, that we need wholeness, and that this path will bring us to a feeling of inner unity and authenticity.

Stories and Complexes

Some time ago, the Italian newspaper I read online every morning published a collection of photographs of a few groups of people, taken throughout their lives. The pictures began in their childhood and progressed through their adolescence, marriages, first child, and so on, until their gray hair appeared. This series of pictures fascinated me, and I looked at it over and over again, seeing several life stories in picture form. The early years of these people showed expressions of beautiful energy, vitality, soft hair, big smiles of joy, innocence, and faces with great expectations for a future that seemed too slow to come. With the progression of the photographs over time, one by one these characteristics began to fade and then vanished. With a sense of dismay, I wondered what happened to that promise, that energy, that vitality? Where did they go? What kinds of events were so dreadful that they melted those vibrant spirits?

I wish I had kept those pictures. They were a graphic illustration of our journey through life. They showed how we face life, fall in love, experience the highs and lows of our existence, and emerge in our unique way. These pictures took on the story of life. The changes taking place in the people reminded me of another story, one of fishermen and travelers, centuries ago. These fishermen and travelers would take their boats, which were frequently their most valued possession, and sail out into the sea to provide a living for their families or to discover new lands and lives. As they set sail, they searched the sky each day to see how the weather was going to be, and they began the journey with high hopes of finding abundant fish for the day. They were capable of meeting many challenges and were confident in their strength and experience. Then slowly, without the sailors' knowing it, remoras, large fish with a dorsal fin that is converted into a suctorial disk, sucked to the bottoms of their boats, sometimes in great numbers. The weight of these fish pulled the boats deeper into the water, slowing their progress, and, in some cases, sinking them. Remoras could bring a drastic end to the hopes and efforts of the fishermen and the explorers, who were terrified of them.

If you stop and think about it, you can imagine how we travel through life in a similar way, with more or less confidence, with more or less strength and courage. Then through the toils and troubles of our lives, we lose our spirit. We forget or perhaps we never even realize that we had or could have dreams and expectations. We let our potentials starve and our visions for a more fulfilling life come to nothing. What is happening to us psychologically is that the weight of our complexes is pulling us down, like remoras attached to a boat.

In the same way that atoms and molecules are the essential components of physical objects, our complexes are the building blocks of our psychic structure. They are also the source

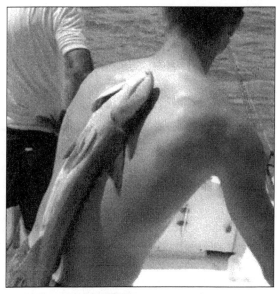

Remora fish with suctorial disk.

41

of our emotional energy. Some of our complexes are positive and some are negative. We are focusing on two of the most negative ones we experience, the negative mother complex and the Death Mother complex, because they hold the most promise for expanding our possibilities and transforming our lives and culture.

Every one of our negative complexes can be like a remora, very destructive and draining of our energy as we struggle to live with or against them. If they are deep enough and strong enough, complexes can cause underlying depression or anxiety that exhausts us in the same way a chronic illness would. Of course, our complexes can show up in our bodies in ways that range from weight problems to breathing problems and from heart problems to other illnesses. Complexes easily disrupt our relationships with ourselves, destroy our self-esteem, and erode the nature of our other relationships. But each of these complexes also holds an inspiring challenge and the promise of transformation, the potential of a greater experience of life.

The stories of our major complexes begin in our deepest human experiences: how we experience our mothers and fathers. They are formed by the emotional encounters that shape us—usually or most notably the negative or traumatic ones, because growing up is always difficult and a struggle, in even the best of circumstances.

We can find the developmental phases of childhood and adolescence delineated by the psychoanalyst Erik Erikson in his book *Identity and the Life Cycle*, in which he indicates that each phase is centered around a crisis. The names he gives these developmental crises in childhood and adolescence reflect their intense and dramatic nature. For example, in infancy, our developmental crisis is labeled "trust versus mistrust," meaning that our sense of trust or mistrust in ourselves, the world, and life is determined when we are tiny. Following this phase are the developmental crises of "autonomy versus shame and doubt," "initiative versus guilt," "industry versus inferiority," "identity versus identity confusion," and "intimacy versus isolation." Every step in growing up presents a major challenge and the potential of traumas. Each trauma can become the root system of a tree of complexes that has many branches. And as you may know, imagine, or suspect, most of

42

these complexes form to protect our vulnerable child-self from shame, guilt, trauma, fear, or some other overwhelming emotion. They also protect us from the more subliminal demands and messages in our early lives, such as "Don't bother me. Don't be stupid. Do it yourself. Please your parents. I wish you weren't here. I wish you were somebody else. Please your teachers," and so on. The few things I've mentioned here don't even approach major traumas, such as violence, abuse, illness, loss of a parent, or having severely disturbed parents.

The complexes that will most affect our lives have to do with relationships, because the way others respond to us as we grow up shapes our view of ourselves and of the world. Once we awaken to a complex, we face a task, a journey. Yet this journey isn't one that will take us "back to normal," for in Jungian terms, there is also a promise. The promise of the journey is to have an enlarged life of increased empowerment and authenticity. It is to free ourselves of the complexes that have been sapping our energy like remoras.

The promise in a complex comes from its archetypal foundation. Archetypes are the psychological blueprints that determine how our experiences and emotions can be channeled. In his essay "The Significance of the Father in the Destiny of the Individual," Jung says, "Man 'possesses' many things which he has never acquired but he has inherited from his ancestors. He is not born a *tabula rasa*, he is merely born unconscious. But he brings with him systems that are organized and ready to function in a specifically human way, and these he owes to millions of years of human development."

So I like to think that archetypes are like hidden magnets in our psyche that attract and pattern our experiences and emotions. For example, if my mother is cold, distant, and secretly hostile to me and shames me for not meeting her expectations, then I will have internalized a fear of abandonment and my whole defense system will have become hypervigilant. It is as if I had been born with my umbilical cord strangling me. We can imagine that as soon as my husband, friend, family member, boss, or colleague makes a negative comment, I freeze. All of the early fear in my body jumps out and seizes me. I deny my own feelings and try to please and accommodate everyone around me. Along with paralysis, I might retreat into silence and a placating attitude, or I might hide emotionally and try to become invisible. On a deeper level, I will have anger, rage, and resentment at the failure of my mother, or whomever else I put in a similar significant role, to value and understand me and to fulfill her archetypal role as a "good enough" mother. In psychological terms, I will have developed a negative mother complex—and in an extreme case such as this one, a Death Mother complex. This complex is how my psyche will organize my emotions and early experiences around the archetype of the negative mother or the Death Mother.

Whenever we perceive we are encountering rejection, coldness, not being valued or understood, this complex will flood us with paralysis, fear, confusion, anger, and resentment. Complexes, the unresolved results of the incidents that gnarled and twisted our growth, affect not only the way we perceive our outer and inner worlds but also how we respond to outer and inner events.

But every archetypal image has two poles. The negative Death Mother has its opposite: the positive Great Mother that offers the greatest value of the feminine archetype. The complex provides the link between the positive archetypal potential and our ego, our conscious personality. So, when we do the work of integrating such a powerful complex, our entire personality will be radically transformed. We will have found new strength, emotional balance, and a new potential for loving and being loved.

Stories That Heal and Transform

Isak Dinesen was a Danish writer who is best known for *Out of Africa*. In one of her finely crafted stories, she writes that "all sorrows can be borne if you put them into a story about them." But doing this is not an easy task, and thinking about our sorrows this way brings back to mind Jung's statement that many of us are stuck against a story we cannot tell. Frequently, we are too overwhelmed by our emotions to face the story. Or we are struggling so hard with our lives that we are unable to articulate our story. Out of fear and in order to survive, we might have buried it so deep that we can't uncover it. Such a story, then, explains how a complex forms and grows, and then the story begins "to tell us." These tales show up in our dreams, our despair, our weeping, our anxiety, and our other troubles in living and getting along with others. And they lurk in our bodies: our weight, hunger, headaches, fatigue, sleeplessness, and a myriad of discomforts and illnesses. Other stories, timeless stories of human experiences, can often help us begin to discover our truth, so that we can become conscious of it and articulate it rather than having it "live us."

Every culture since the beginning of time has existed on its stories. They can support, shape, and lead us into the kind of healing and growth that is close to the heart of our feminine nature. When we read myths and fairy tales, if we let ourselves step into their world of poetry and imagination, we step out of the rational, concrete, patriarchal world of our time and into the symbolic life. In this way, we become receptive to our inner environment, and as a result, we will learn that these stories are like sacred revelations. These old myths and tales reflect the structures of our lives today. And they describe how the energies of life, our archetypal patterns, are living through us. Examining them teaches us about intimacy with ourselves: how we are structured and how we can accept that we must face seemingly insoluble problems, unbearable realities, and the nature of our deepest longings. While we may have thought fairy tales can be fun to read with our children, which they can, they can also help us uncover, tell, and live out who we really are. And as we are working to become more conscious of our story, fairy tales can help us move from being unconsciously lived by the dramatic structures of our complexes to seeing the solutions that will help us transform our lives and create a new version of ourselves. Later in the book I will share this process in full, but for now, let us take a brief look at how fairy tales helped the people we presented as examples—Timothy, Erin, and Andrea—clarify how their negative mother or Death Mother complexes got started.

Jung is right when he tells us that in many cases, "The patient who comes to us has a story that needs to be told, and which as a rule no one knows of." So the story, which is often the narrative of our dominant complex, needs to be discovered. And because it is such a powerful, hidden story, we also need to uncover the major emotions that are secreted away as the integral parts of it. But neither the truth nor insight alone sets us free. As we put together our chronicle and highlight antidotes, dramas, and feelings, we need to disclose our story to someone who cares—someone who doesn't know all the answers but who cares and has experienced his or her own journey through this territory. When we begin this journey, it is very humbling for all of us to admit that "I do not really know what I feel. I do not say what I mean, and, all too often, I do not do what I say."

When I began working with Timothy, I asked him if he had a favorite fairy tale. The only tale he recalled from childhood was of Hansel and Gretel. His memory was vague, and he asked, "Weren't they lost in the woods?" Then we began putting the pieces of the fairy tale together. They were the children of a poor woodcutter living in the forest. Their mother insisted that she and her husband abandon the children in the woods, because the family was so impoverished there was enough food for only her and her husband to survive.

Soon the symbolism of the tale began to emerge, and it became apparent that the term *impoverished* meant "emotionally impoverished." At this point, Timothy was able to observe that the children's being deep in the forest could also mean they were unconscious. Once we reached the part of the story when the children found their way home again, and their mother had to insist upon abandoning them a second time, he was easily able to make the connection with his own story. Timothy was emotionally abandoned by a father lost in his work *and* a mother driven to find some kind of recognition or value in her social life. His parents were so cut off from their feelings, wounded, needy, or narcissistic that he was abandoned from the beginning. Where was love? Timothy's children were dear to him, but he didn't know how to show his love or to let them love him.

Like Timothy, many of us walk easily into the witch's gingerbread house. After all, feeding on materialism and thinking that having enough money could make everyone in our life happy is an easy temptation. Many of us are still stuck in that house.

46

The fairy tale helped Timothy realize that even though he had all the material things he needed, he was an emotionally abandoned child. As our work continued, we needed to develop how this abandonment affected him psychologically and emotionally—how the loneliness, the insecurity, the fear, and, at a deeper level, the anger became part of his secret story, the story of his negative mother complex.

Erin's story was a different matter. She had always been fascinated with "Cinderella." This tale had stayed on her mind for years because she identified with being stuck in the ashes, a familiar position that many of us may identify with. But as we explored the tale's opening, we saw that Cinderella's mother was dying, and she instructed Cinderella to always be good and pious. I wondered with Erin if this could mean that her mother was a good mother to her when she was good and pious, in other words, when she pleased her mother. You may recall that Erin was a pediatric nurse, a confessed perfectionist, and a pleaser who had been overtaken by a general feeling of unhappiness. Her mother had also been a dynamic, successful woman, driven by anxiety. Erin was expected to go along and perform many of the household tasks to support her mother and, no wonder, was rarely considered personally by her parents.

Stepmothers in fairy tales frequently suggest the absence of the good enough mother and the presence of a cold, narcissistic mother. As we worked through the story, Erin compared her life with this tale and saw how the tale reflected her early experiences. She was diminished as a person, given mundane tasks, and was unappreciated even though she became accommodating and helpful. Erin realized that she had to confront the bad mother that she had internalized from childhood. Additionally, she began to see that the culture had supported her mother's becoming a financial success. The culture did not, however, offer Erin's mother similar support for becoming self-aware or whole, and therefore the financial success she achieved came at the expense of her children's emotional well-being. It also became clear to both of us that the negative half-sisters in the fairy tale could represent the self-critical, self-diminishing inner voices that Erin had developed growing up, which helped drive her to be a perfectionist and a pleaser. Finding herself in the story increased Erin's understanding of her life and her compassion for herself. Further, it helped her see that an important part of our work would be to develop her relationship with the positive mothering capacity within herself. This is the capacity to nurture, hold, comfort, and love herself as well as to nourish her own growth. This capacity is represented by the trees, birds, and nature and, in some versions of the story, by the fairy godmother.

Finally, let's examine an even more dramatic example of the Death Mother at work in a person's life. Andrea, you will recall, had been depressed most of her life. Her mother was an alcoholic who had a nervous breakdown. And because Andrea's father had to work in another town, Andrea was left with the responsibility not only of her brother and sister but also of her mother. Andrea had read several Jungian books on fairy tales and she identified the most with "The Handless Maiden." She felt that the family's poverty, her mother's total incapacity, and her father's absence had left her with no choices in her early life; she had been robbed of her childhood and the things she needed as a child. She also chose to be the good and responsible one, by even taking care of her mother. I could easily understand why she identified with being "handless," but I had trouble seeing how her life was reflected by the rest of the story.

In the story, a miller and his wife came on hard times, and a man, the devil, stepped out from behind a tree and offered the miller riches for what stood behind the mill. The miller naively agreed, not realizing that his own daughter was standing behind the mill. The man said he would come in three years to claim what was his. When the devil returned, the girl wept so much that the devil couldn't come near her, and the tears ran down her arms and hands. The devil required her father to chop off her hands. Still she wept so much that he was repulsed and left. At that moment, the girl's journey of healing began.

Andrea felt her parents had taken the easy way out, as the miller did, rather than facing their own reality. The girl's tears reflected the endless tears that Andrea had repressed and that were at the source of her depression. The passivity of the wife in the story and how the father neglected to consult her reminded Andrea of her mother's passivity and illness and her father's neglect of her mother.

An insightful person, Andrea saw the miller and the devil as larger societal forces that urge us to take the easy way out and seek our answers in materialism and what looks like a good life. She wondered if this tale could also be speaking to us collectively about how the patriarchy, our unconscious dominant value system, is "selling out" our time and blinding us to our needs for truly caring about ourselves, others, and love. Are we selling out the feminine principle and the needs, values, and nourishment in its potentials to the devil of productivity and practicality? As women, we should ask ourselves, how can a woman love her children—or her husband or partner for that matter—in a healthy way if she can't love herself or life? How can children grow up to be capable of love when our society abandons them? I also see the Death Mother's societal influence in Andrea's case: In our world, people who, like Andrea's parents, are suffering from breakdowns, alcoholism, poor job prospects, or other adversities are left abandoned, for the most part, by the rest of us.

The primary benefit of Andrea's locating herself in this story was that she realized she was not alone. The fairy tale told her that she was part of an archetypal story, one that many people experience in various forms. This fact brought her hope because the tale outlines a timeless human path to healing and transformation.

Fairy tales help us get a perspective on our situation. They describe in symbolic terms how our situation and our dominant complex came into being and evolved. Then the tale, as we will see, becomes a symbolic expression of our personal quest toward a more fulfilled life. Fairy tales also show us how symbolic thinking can help us understand ourselves. Later in the book, we will see how fairy tales can aid our personal search for healing and transformation.

As we approach the next chapter and the story of Medusa, I want to say a few words about dreams and myths. I always enjoy dreams in which a baby has been born or a new child appears. Such dreams help me feel the wonder and the hopefulness that surrounds new life. They also invite me to accept new potentials with a sense of awe and commitment. The myth of Medusa is another kind of dream: a collective dream expressing the depth of our experiences over time. Though the settings have changed since this myth evolved, our patterns of living and conflicts are continuing reflections of the archetypal motifs mirrored in this old story, the symbols of which can help us understand ourselves.

We endanger our own possibilities for wholeness and a satisfying life when we demean our mythological heritage as primitive fables, fantasies, or statements about life that aren't really true. The same thing happens when we diminish the significance of our night visions by saying, "I was only dreaming." Dreams and myths take us into the dark world of our personal and cultural unconscious, where the roots of the continuing oppression and the spiritual imprisonment of lives lie. If we are willing to look, ready to see whatever may appear, and if we will listen to the voices stirring within us, we will find that out of our transpersonal depths, the gifts of understanding and transformation are at hand.

The myth of Medusa is a collective dream that is very different from my dream of new life. This collective dream shows how the darkness of a major complex descends. It is the dark before the light. But as the myth proceeds, it will bring transformation and the power of the light into reality, nourishing, fostering, and strengthening new life.

PART
TWO

A Healing Path

The great work of our time is to bring the feminine into this culture.
And it is not an easy path. How does each one of us contribute?
Believe it or not, it's done in the most personal ways. Take time to listen to
your dreams. Write them down. Take time to recognize that there are things
going on within you that need to be felt, or said, or lived, or grieved.
Pay attention to these things both in yourself and in the people in your life.
Pay attention to the authentic self.

– MARION WOODMAN

Chapter 4

FROM PARALYSIS TO FULL VITALITY
THE MYTH OF MEDUSA

These are the stories that never, never die, that are carried like seed into a
new country, are told to you and me and make us new and lasting strengths.

— MERIDEL LE SUEUR

The Death Mother supports an inner and outer patriarchal system
that haunts a woman with feelings of failure and worthlessness and
oppresses men with feelings of depression and dissatisfaction with their
lives. This complex, like the remora, feeds on us, saps our energy, drains
our vitality, drags us down, and paralyzes us. Regrettably, the majority of
people have little understanding of or connection with their unconscious
and suffer the difficult consequences of the darkest, most destructive
power of the feminine archetype without understanding it.

Thinking about these wounds, their effects, and our tendency to be
unconscious to the deeper energies shaping our lives reminds me of a
significant instance from a trip in my early adulthood. About forty years
ago, a large group of friends and I went from Italy to Greece for the
summer. We enjoyed camping on a beach that was a little less than an
hour's drive from Athens. This beach was a quiet, simple place, and the
only house nearby belonged to one of the fisherman that provided us
with wonderful meals. We also became friendly with the few people who
lived in a little neighboring village. Even though we didn't understand
their language very well, we enjoyed the pleasure of singing and dancing

the sirtaki with them at night. When it was time for us to leave for home, the people gathered around us for a final farewell. As we stood together, a woman seized my hand as if she wanted to lead me somewhere before we left. She was older, thin, energetic, and dressed in black. She had deep, piercing eyes. Because of the language barrier, she began speaking more loudly in Greek. She also began waving her hands to make sweeping gestures, emphasizing that she wanted me to come into her bakery.

We were all frustrated because we could not understand what she was saying and because we needed to leave. Yet it seemed that I was caught in the middle, and if I wanted to put this situation to an end, I would have to follow her without knowing where she was leading me. Of course, my "friends" in the group started teasing me by saying things like, "The witch wants to cook you in her oven" or "You know you are going in, but you don't know if you are getting out." They certainly didn't help strengthen my trust and confidence. At last, I decided to accept her offer, but I took a male friend with me for protection.

Bravely, we entered her little bakery. We passed her counter and went into the back, where her old oven was. The oven had a beautiful oval shape. It was made of stone and was centuries old. It had a small opening in the front, where you could see the fires burning. On the side of the oven was a small door. As my friend and I stared at the door, I was startled to see that there was a carefully sculpted face of the Medusa looking back at me.

I felt scared and trapped, just as Hansel in the fairy tale must have felt right before the witch put him in the oven. But I tried to stay composed, to maintain a calm appearance, and to hope for the best. In fact, I soon saw that this Greek woman, dressed in black, was very proud of her oven and that her intentions were kindly. She had prepared a bag of breads and cookies for us to take on our trip home. We left her bakery with a big sigh of relief and touched by her lovely generosity. But I also had feelings of guilt for having fallen into the trap of terror, which had quickly opened in me like an abyss.

This abyss is the next place we are going to explore. This very dark wound that is in most of us and that this woman, who I initially thought looked like a fairy tale witch, touched in me. This is the wound of the

Medusa that lies deep in the cave of our psyche, ready to paralyze us. We need to look at this destructive aspect of the feminine that lives within us and destroys our vitality and creativity with her paralyzing powers.

We must remember that as important as our thinking intellect, rationality, and even willpower are to our lives, they cannot bring about our healing and transformation. The essence of all our religions, from the most primitive to the most highly sophisticated, has always been expressed by our souls in stories, parables, and myths. The Christian Mass itself is a symbolic drama telling the great story of death, transformation, resurrection, and a new way of life. No matter what we think we believe, no matter what doctrine we espouse—religious or psychological—we will not be transformed without deeply experiencing the meanings of our beliefs in some personal, symbolic manner that leads us to change how we are living. The myth of Medusa is an extraordinary mythic story from our collective past. What it can tell us today is as sacred as any religious parable. This myth is a symbolic story of how the patriarchy has abused and banished the feminine, how it can be redeemed, and the tremendous healing and instinctual power that can be freed in this process. As you will see, the bridge enabling us to make this great story relevant to our own healing, growth, and freedom is the Jungian perspective. The Jungian point of view is that our most troublesome complexes, which result from the wounds that shaped us, also hold a promise. Jung considered complexes to be the "royal road" to our unconscious and the architect of symptoms, dreams, and a transformed life. A myth like this one will show us what has been wounded, how the wound occurred, and the suffering such a wound inflicts. And we will then see what must be healed within ourselves by dying and being transformed and, finally, what new potentials we must live.

The Myth of Medusa

The mythic story of Medusa gives us many clues that can help us understand what has happened to the feminine principle in our society. Much of what we know about Medusa comes from the Roman poet

Ovid. Ovid's major work was his *Metamorphoses,* a collection of over 250 myths that chronicle the history of the world from its creation to the deification of Julius Caesar. The Latin title, *Metamorphoseon libri,* means "books of transformation," and this meaning reveals the underlying theme of transformation in these myths.

When the myth of Medusa begins, we find her to be a strikingly beautiful young woman with alluring eyes and elegant, flowing hair. As mythic stories often go, she was the daughter of a king and queen: King Phorcys and Queen Ceto. Both of her parents had semidivine characteristics, which means they were connected to the far-reaching sources of life. Her father, King Phorcys, was known as one of the "old men of the sea." Their kingdom was a series of islands at the far side of the ocean, close to the end of the world and the entrance to the Kingdom of the Dead. In this initial setting, we can see symbolically that this myth is positioned in a special place that likewise suggests transformation.

Medusa and two of her sisters were mythological creatures called the Gorgons. Her first Gorgon sister was Stheno, whose name means "strength." Her second Gorgon sister was Euryale, and her name means, strangely enough, "reaching across the sea." Although Medusa was beautiful, she was mortal. Stheno and Euryale were immortal, but they were hideous. The ancient Greek mytho-historian Hesiod, who described them in his *Theogony,* portrayed them with scaly bodies, wings, claws, and frightening teeth.

Medusa's name means "she who dominates or rules," as well as "protectress" or "guardian." Her beauty and her splendid hair made her a commanding presence in almost every circumstance, and by the time she was a young woman, Medusa was proud of her beauty and vain about her magnificent hair. Ovid explained that she was "astonishingly fair" and was pursued by many jealous suitors. We may easily imagine that a woman with such outstanding characteristics will soon be getting into trouble with the gods and goddesses of antiquity.

On one of the main islands where Medusa lived, there was a special temple dedicated to the goddess Athena. Athena was no ordinary goddess. According to the Jungian analyst Jean Shinoda Bolen, in her book *Goddesses in Everywoman,* Athena was the goddess who sided with the patriarchy. She had sprung full-grown from the head of her father, Zeus, emitting a mighty war cry. Athena considered herself to have only one parent, the father god, Zeus. In his book *Goddesses: Mysteries of the Feminine Divine*, the mythologist Joseph Campbell depicts Athena's birth from the head of Zeus as an example of the patriarchal culture's assimilation of the goddess. Athena was the only goddess always clothed in armor and pictured with the visor of her helmet open to show her beauty. She was also a virgin goddess, the guide and protector of heroes, the goddess of wisdom and craft, who was ruled by her head rather than her heart. Athena's basic characteristics were her power, her wisdom, and the masculinity of her origins. But she was also a very jealous goddess, and she became furious with Medusa for boasting that she was more beautiful than Athena.

Often in the old Greek myths, beautiful women attract the patriarchal gods, who seek to ravish and dominate them. Again, we might imagine that these acts are examples of the growing patriarchal culture trying to assimilate and control the transformative aspects of the feminine. Frequently, these situations turn out badly for the women who are involved. But as we will see in the myth of Medusa, if we look beyond the surface of these situations, we find they can also lead to deeper and more complicated transformations. In this myth, Poseidon, the brother of Zeus and god of the sea, lusted after Medusa. Symbolically, Poseidon, like all of the Greek gods, is a complicated image, full of darkness and light. His darker side is evident in this myth. According to Jean Shinoda Bolen in her book *Gods in Everyman*, Poseidon is a metaphor for the part of the patriarchal archetype that lost out to Zeus and is repressed in our culture and in men who work at keeping everything rational and under control. When emotions are bottled up in a person or in a society, they will become a psychological complex that will attack and seek to dominate the feminine, both within ourselves and within our society. In this sense, Poseidon is dangerous, vindictive, and destructive as a metaphor of the repressed emotionality of the patriarchy, just as he was violent in his love affairs.

Poseidon tried many tricks in his pursuit of Medusa, such as turning himself into a bird and a horse. When he was able to finally corner her in Athena's magnificent temple on the main island of her family's kingdom, he overpowered and raped her. When Athena heard of this event, she was very offended that her temple had been violated in this way. But because she couldn't stand the pride Medusa took in her own beauty—after all, as the goddess of war, reason, and intellect, Athena was more majestic than beautiful—and because she was a daughter of the patriarchy, Athena blamed Medusa and not Poseidon. We might wonder as well if Athena, the virgin goddess, was equally offended by the commission of any sex act, which she had never experienced, in her temple.

In retaliation, Athena turned Medusa into a dreadful monster. Medusa's lovely, flowing hair turned into a tangle of horrifying, hissing snakes. Her alluring eyes become large and fiery. Replacing her captivating mouth were swollen lips with a large tongue dangling from them, and under her flared nostrils were enormous fangs shaped like the tusks of a wild boar. Medusa's appearance was now so terrifying that anyone who saw her turned into stone. At this point, Medusa was banished into a large cave near the end of the earth, which might also mean psychologically that what she symbolizes is repressed out of our ordinary conscious awareness.

While all of this was taking place, another saga was developing in the area: the myth of Perseus. Perseus was an emerging hero, and his journey and encounter with Medusa would further the process of transformation and growth being illustrated by both myths. Eventually the myth of Perseus will help teach us how we can heal and transform the Death Mother complex that can paralyze us so easily.

The circumstances of Perseus's birth were intriguing, especially in contrast to Medusa's ravishment by Poseidon, which did not result in a birth or a creative outcome. The mother of Perseus was Danaë, the beautiful daughter of Acrisius, the king of Argos. When Danaë was a child, an oracle predicted that she would bear a son who would kill her father, King Acrisius. As the king desperately tried to keep this prophecy from coming true, and to prevent Danaë from having children, he shut her off from the world. In early versions of the myth, he enclosed her in a brazen underground chamber in his palace. In a later version, the Roman poet Horace changed her prison to a brazen tower, and this version of the myth has become the accepted tradition. Of course, shutting her away from human men did not protect her from the attention of Zeus, the most powerful father god, who was lord of the sky, the rain, and the clouds and who wielded the awful thunderbolt.

The early Zeus was a father god, a patriarchal god who had to overcome his own powerful father, the god Cronus, in order to claim his place on Mount Olympus. He also had to battle and defeat the Titans, the great nature forces, in order to consolidate his ruling position. In Greek mythology, the image of Zeus as the father god evolved over time. Initially, he stood for power, organization, and creativity. The early Zeus was inexorable and harsh, but over time, he seemed to learn benevolence, wisdom, and maturity. Secure in his power, he became the supreme, benevolent father of gods and mortals. In this role, he often showed up as a mentor as well as a protector of women and children and of culture.

However, he was still a seeker of beautiful women, and we might think of his drive in this direction in archetypal terms. I believe this persistent desire symbolizes the dominant masculine principle's wish to unite with the transformative, creative aspects of the feminine principle. In this situation, Zeus's approach to Danaë contrasts sharply with Poseidon's pursuit of Medusa. Zeus found Danaë imprisoned by her father, and he came upon her as a shower of gold and impregnated her. This was a much gentler and more poetic approach than the way Poseidon ravished Medusa in the temple of a goddess that he was in conflict with. It was also a creative approach, as he came in a shower of gold, signifying great value, and their encounter left Danaë pregnant with her future son and hero, Perseus. Danaë was able to keep her son's presence secret from her father for several years, until finally King Acrisius heard him playing. The king refused to believe that Perseus was the son of Zeus, or perhaps this claim made Acrisius even more afraid for his life. In any case, to protect himself, Acrisius acted quickly and placed Danaë and the child Perseus in a wooden chest and set it adrift in the Aegean Sea. In this way, he sought to get rid of them without being responsible for the murder of his daughter and grandson.

Fortunately for Danaë and Perseus, Zeus protected them and guided their chest across the Aegean Sea to the island of Seriphus. As the chest washed up on the beach, it was discovered by the fisherman, Diktys, and he rescued them. The fisherman is also an archetypal figure and often symbolizes our ability to gain valuable aspects of ourselves from the symbolic sea that represents our unconscious and our inner depths. Diktys took Danaë and Perseus to meet his brother—the island's king, Polydectes—and they were welcomed to the island.

As time passed, Perseus, who was to become one of the Greeks' greatest heroes, grew to be handsome, strong, and courageous. While Perseus was growing up, King Polydectes was falling in love with Danaë and pressed her to marry him. But Danaë did not love him and devoted her attention to her son. Once again, from a psychological standpoint, we are running into an interesting archetypal and symbolic situation. On the archetypal level in myths that symbolize the deeper structures of our lives, the son, particularly when the father is absent, represents the inner quest for the mother or, in a more general sense, for the archetypal feminine. As the myths of Perseus and Medusa come together, we will see how this joining brings transformation, healing, and a new experience of life and empowerment to the wounded feminine principle.

At this point in the myth, Polydectes, a powerful king, could have taken Danaë by force, but he was wary of her now formidable son. Still, Polydectes never stopped scheming to have her. Eventually, the king came up with a wily trap for Perseus. Polydectes announced his intention to marry the daughter of a neighboring king. In celebration of the betrothal, Polydectes arranged for a banquet. Tradition required guests to such banquets to bring a wedding present, and Polydectes asked each guest to bring a horse as a gift. This request left Perseus in a bind because he didn't have a horse and he had no money of his own to buy one. In all likelihood, Polydectes hoped that Perseus would be shamed into leaving the island. Instead of fleeing, however, Perseus naively promised to bring the king anything else that he desired—even the head of Medusa. Polydectes, with his scheme to win Danaë still cleverly disguised, eagerly accepted Perseus's offer to bring him the head of Medusa. The king knew that no man had survived an encounter with Medusa. He hoped that with Perseus's death, his mother would be grief stricken, alone, and without comfort and then would seek solace in marrying him.

The gravity of the bold adventure soon became clear to Perseus. In despair, he wandered for many days until he ended up in a lonely part of Seriphus. Like many mythological heroes, Perseus seemed called upon to do the impossible. But he will succeed because of the help he receives from other supernatural powers. We, too, often feel lonely and lost when we are facing a life that isn't working and changing seems impossible. When we understand these myths symbolically, however, we realize they are teaching us to keep going and to be open to forces and strengths deep within us that can help and guide us in the journey of transforming our lives.

Of course, defeating the powerful Medusa seemed like an unthinkable project. Perseus would first have to enter her lair without being detected. Then to avoid being turned into stone, he would have to slay her without looking into her face. But that wasn't all. Having achieved his goal, he would then have to flee with incredible speed in order to avoid the swift, vengeful pursuit of her winged Gorgon sisters.

While Perseus was in despair, Athena, the patron goddess and protector of heroes, appeared to him. Of course, she already hated Medusa and gladly gave Perseus permission to kill her. She also assured Perseus that she would keep him under her protection. To assist his efforts further, she presented him with a polished bronze shield that would enable him to see the mirrored image of Medusa in it, thus avoiding the direct sight of her. Then Athena counseled him as to how to proceed. Moreover, he was met by Hermes, the messenger of Zeus and crosser of boundaries. Hermes knew that Perseus was favored by Athena and Zeus, and he had carefully observed his development into manhood. Hermes gave Perseus the final weapon that he would need to kill Medusa, a sword made of adamant, a metallic stone so hard that it was unbreakable. However, Athena and Hermes were still afraid that these weapons were not enough. They suggested to Perseus that he should get additional help and magic objects from the nymphs. But Athena and Hermes did not know where to find the nymphs, so they told Perseus to ask the Graeae and to be aware that he would have to trick them into answering him.

Perseus then traveled to the mountain on which Atlas stood, supporting the world. There he found the cave of the Graeae. The Graeae were referred to as the "old ones" because they had been born old with gray hair. They were also the older sisters of the Gorgons. The Graeae had the bodies of swans and had only a single tooth and a single eye between them. In order to eat, they had to pass the single tooth from one to the other, and in order to see, they had to do the same thing with their single eye. We may imagine the Graeae represent our old attitudes that have a limited perspective and no aptitude for change. It takes an act of consciousness to trick them into helping with a new direction. Once Perseus arrived at their cave, he hid and waited for a moment when one of them was passing the single eye to her sister. This was the only time they were blind. Taking advantage of this situation, Perseus snatched their eye and offered to give it back if they would tell him where the kingdom of the nymphs was, and specifically how to find the nymphs. Once he had gained this information, he flung their eye into Lake Tritonis in order to prevent them from warning their sisters, the Gorgons.

When he found the nymphs, who lived nearby, they gave him three important aids for his task: winged sandals, which would allow him to approach and later escape the Gorgon's lair with great speed; the cap of darkness, or the cap of Hades, which made the wearer invisible; and a pouch or knapsack in which to put his trophy, Medusa's head, so that he could carry it safely away. Once again, it is interesting to note the meaning in these events when we look at them symbolically. Joseph Campbell writes in his book *Goddesses: Mysteries of the Feminine Divine* that in these Greek myths of heroes' journeys, the hero's principal transformative experiences or the tools for the hero's transformative experiences are with or from the nymphs—"that is to say, the feminine principle."

Now well-equipped for his journey—his sword in his belt, his bag over his shoulder, and his shield on his arm—Perseus swiftly flew, invisible, to the island where Medusa and her Gorgon sisters lived. It was at the end of the earth, where neither the sun nor moon ever shone. Once there, he began to make his way to Medusa's cave. In psychology, such symbolism shows that it is frequently in the depths and hidden recesses of our unconscious that our best resources are forged. In other words, we have to dare to think the impossible.

As Perseus was traveling the roads and passing fields, he saw frightening shapes of men and animals whom the terrifying sight of Medusa had turned to stone. After locating Medusa's cave, he carefully entered it to begin his search. He steadily advanced into the depths of the cavern. Continuing to follow Athena's instructions, he walked backward and held his polished bronze shield on his left arm, at an angle that enabled him to use the reflections in the shield to see where he was going. As he pushed forward into the shadowy tunnels, he suddenly saw the dreadful form of Medusa reflected on his shield. When Perseus was close enough to the horrifying creature, he seized the sword given to him by Hermes, and with a single blow, he cut off her head. Even after the killing blow, the angry snakes of her hair tried to attack and envelop him. He powerfully avoided entanglement with them, seized Medusa's head, and thrust it into the sack that had been given to him by the nymphs. From the gushing blood of Medusa sprang the magic, winged horse Pegasus: a forceful symbol of soaring, new instinctual life. So did the giant Chrysaor, holding his golden sword. Chrysaor was known as He of the Golden Sword and was another symbol of strength, vitality, and value. The blood dripping from Medusa's wounds was collected in two vials, which Athena then gave to the god of healing, Asclepius. One of the vials contained a deadly poison, and the other one contained a healing potion believed to be powerful enough to bring the dead back to life.

The fury of the struggle awakened the two sisters of Medusa, who then tried to follow Perseus and kill him. But using the cap of invisibility that the nymphs had given him, he was able to escape, flying quickly away from that gloomy and hostile island. In psychological terms, we can interpret this part of the myth to mean that we must not doubt or regress. Rather, we must keep strongly attached to our new prize of transformed consciousness. With his trophy securely in hand, Perseus flew on his winged sandals back toward Seriphus and home. Yet his journey home from the land of Medusa was a long one, and he encountered many adventures along the way. On his final arrival, he used Medusa's head to turn Polydectes and his followers to stone, freeing his mother. He returned his magic objects to the gods and nymphs and gave Medusa's head to Athena, who set it in the middle of her shield.

After the myth became well-known, it carried great power in the culture of the ancient Greeks. Warriors often painted Medusa's head on their shields to express their ferocity. In his *Metamorphoses,* Ovid goes on to tell us that during Perseus's journeys, he got into an uneven wrestling match with the giant Atlas and "turned around with his back to Atlas, lifted up with his left hand Medusa's head, at which point, the giant turned into a mountain"—the mountain that supports the world.

In chapter 6, we will begin to look at how the symbols, the paradoxes, and the patterns in this story can tell us more about the nature of who we are; how we are experiencing the destructive, paralyzing power of the Death Mother; and how we can transform the wounded feminine within ourselves into vitality and creativity. But first, let us explore the psychological context of the issues we are confronting as the starting point for our journey into the transforming power of the myth of Medusa.

Chapter 5

POWER, REALITY, THE FEMININE, AND PROJECTIONS

Paradox is the essence of living.
Perhaps the greatest paradox in the human psyche is our longing for union,
for peace, for solutions, though experience has taught us that it is our
conflicts and our failures which are in fact our points of growth.

– Irene Claremont de Castillejo

Before we delve further into the myth of Medusa, let's consider some of the ways Jungian psychology looks at the feminine and masculine principles in our makeup and at the archetypal patterns that channel these instinctual energies within us. These reflections will help create a framework for exploring the meanings of this myth in order to heal and reimagine our lives.

For many years, our search for the meaning and the experience of the feminine has been like looking for some lost object in the dark. In many ways, we haven't known what we are trying to find and we haven't understood the depth and complexity of our challenge. But it is reassuring to know that we, men and women, are on this quest together; that we are being compelled to undertake it; and that we are making progress. Throughout this book, we are taking a fresh look at ideas that have been simmering for decades or longer and that continue to change our perspectives and open our lives to a future that we could not have imagined previously.

65

Jung's perspective on our psychological nature has awakened so many of us to the potentials of understanding ourselves and reinventing our lives from the inside out. Nowhere has his work been more helpful than in his definition of the feminine principle and its place in our personalities and lives.

In general, Jung used the word *Eros* to describe what he considered the feminine principle. Eros is the mythological god of love and son of the goddess of love, Aphrodite. As a psychic aspect in both men and women, Eros reflects our capacity to love life, ourselves, and each other, and it values our ability to love. It provides the foundation that allows us to know and understand each other, to care about each other, and to experience compassion. The Jungian concept of Eros denotes personal relatedness, a keen interest in relationships, and a prevailing attitude that works for conciliation and reconciliation. Eros evokes self-integration, subjectivity, and the concern for individuals, and it is rooted in the material universe and the earthly feminine qualities, such as accepting, yielding, experiencing, and being receptive.

We can understand Jung's ideas about the feminine and masculine sides of our personalities by considering human biology. Just as every man has the X, or female, chromosome and female hormones, he also has a group of psychological characteristics that make up a minority feminine element in his personality. A woman, likewise, has a minority masculine component in her psychological makeup (Jung, *Collected Works*, vol. 9i, para. 512). Jung uses the terms *masculine* and *feminine* to denote age-old principles, much as the alchemists and Eastern mystics did. That is to say, in a Jungian context these terms describe archetypal principles rather than cultural roles or stereotypes. Therefore, in normal development, each woman has a predominantly feminine personality with a complementary masculine component and each man has a predominantly masculine personality with a complementary feminine component. Of course, women and men come in many varieties, and Jung's theory is not meant to limit the roles and lifestyles of men and women and how they express themselves. The man's feminine side Jung calls the *anima,* and the woman's masculine side he calls the *animus.*

In his *Red Book*, Jung recalls the encounter with his own anima, whom he calls Salome. He concludes from these experiences that his previous lack of a conscious relationship with his anima, his own feminine side, had caused him to experience a life that had lost its energy. This lack of engagement with his feeling self and with life in general—what we might conclude was a depression—forced him to stop and look at himself.

In his book *Jung and the Story of Our Time* (p. 212), Laurens van der Post makes an essential point: Jung thought that our culture's denial of the archetypal feminine and of the feminine's supreme value of love is turning our history into a wasteland. This denial of the feminine, Jung believed, sickens us in mind and spirit, isolates and bewilders us, and gives us the "loss of soul" reflected in our rejection of this great principle within ourselves. When a man loses his relationship to his anima and a society loses its relationship to the feminine, he and we lose our real relationship to life, to love, and to our sources of purpose and meaning. Consequently, we ignore our deep human longing for love and for meaning.

You may remember from my discussion in chapter 1 that the Great Mother is associated with the feminine principle. The Jungian analyst Erich Neumann explained that the Great Mother archetype has two essential positive characteristics. The attributes of the first, or elementary, characteristic are to nourish and protect, to give warmth and security. The second, or transformative, characteristic is defined by the dynamic element of nature, which has an inherent urge toward growth and transformation. Both of Neumann's characteristics are further differentiations of the feminine principle of Eros.

I also shared with you the ideas Singer describes in "The Sadness of the Successful Woman," in which she identifies a basic split that women face in our times and that also affects the feminine in men. This dichotomy has to do with the liberation of women, who have sought equal respect, pay, and opportunities in our patriarchal society. This struggle represents a freeing of the woman's masculine side, our animus, our ability to be self-reliant, independent, autonomous, and successful, as our culture defines that term. Of course, this liberation is long overdue and not yet complete. But there is a very important question for us to ask ourselves at this point. What happens to us, both women and men, when the feminine principle in our culture is being denied and denigrated and our greatest value of love is being sacrificed to overriding patriarchal values, such as success and productivity? Then we all experience the emptiness and sadness Singer is talking about. We are liberating our empowerment, yet at the same time, we are denying our inherent abilities to like, nourish, and take loving care of ourselves and to make the love of ourselves, others, and life the dominant value we try to live by.

We have put the value of love—of life, self, and others—in combative opposition to the value of personal empowerment. In actuality, these two values should be more like the Eastern concepts of Yang and Yin, which are not combative. Rather, they complement each other as opposites while retaining their own identities, reaching toward a universal harmony. Love needs empowerment to have strength and substance, and empowerment needs love in order to have value, purpose, and meaning. We cannot reconcile this split on a personal level until we heal the feminine within ourselves and our society. And in order to heal the feminine, we must transform our Death Mother complex, which leads back to our exploration of the Medusa myth. As we can see by Perseus's shield, which acts as a mirror for him, projections are an important part of this myth. A look at the psychological meaning of projections will aid our exploration and beginning efforts to heal the feminine.

The Evil Eye—Understanding Projections

Understanding projections—how and why we make them and how we can learn and grow from them—is essential in learning how to revalue the feminine in our lives and how to find the golden potentials in the darkness of our Death Mother complex. Projections explain many of the emotional thickets in which we often find ourselves entangled. While most of us have a passing knowledge of the word projection as it is used in psychology, we may not be familiar with where projections come from and how they work. And so we are deprived of the kind of knowledge that could help heal our lives and broaden our growth.

As an example of how projections work on an individual level, let's remember the discord between Timothy and his ex-wife, whom he was unable to confront. The cause of his passivity may have been that although he despised his wife, he would have been ashamed to admit such an ugly emotion to himself. He had to maintain his image as a good person. One way to unconsciously deal with his shame and anger was to say, "I don't despise her—she despises me. Just look at how she treats me." By projecting his disdain onto her, he disowned it in himself. This allowed him to maintain his "good" self-image while denying his shadow, the darker side of himself, which in some instances could have given him the strength and aggressiveness to protect his inner integrity. Only through reflecting upon how we are living and what we are feeling can we begin to recognize who and what we truly are and what we are really doing.

To understand our projections, we also need to understand our shadow, as it is one of the primary sources of our projections. In the development of our personalities and identities, we go through a process of selecting certain portions of our personality that become our favored way of dealing with the world. These propensities are usually based on what we perceive as social norms and are reinforced by our parents and social institutions. The most powerful influences on how we choose to relate to the world are the early experiences of our mother, and later the experiences of both our mother and father. During the process of development, other qualities that could have been part of our conscious personality, but did not fit the perceived norms or promote our feelings of emotional safety, are rejected and repressed into the shadow, or dark side of our personality.

For example, Timothy's early life was so emotionally impoverished that he repressed his feelings, wants, and needs in order to feel safe. By doing this, he also repressed his ability to stand up for himself in personal relationships. In another example, Erin, the pediatric nurse, in the face of a demanding mother, became kind, loving, and accommodating and repressed her ability to be strong enough to seek what she really needed in life and from other people. Or Andrea, who had to endure an almost impossible life during her whole childhood, went on to achieve a lot. But she had repressed her ability to love and enjoy life because she couldn't even think about being loved and happy in her childhood. Timothy, Erin, and Andrea, like many of us, had also repressed their abilities to have the great emotions that we need to confront ourselves and life. One wonders how Timothy's life might have been different if he had been able to get furious with his wife and confront her earlier in their marriage. Our shadow also includes the complexes we are not aware of. The processes work within us, guiding and shaping our perceptions without our being conscious of their influences. Our shadow also contains our unlived potentials, which may appear as unacceptable to us, particularly because they may be emotions and attitudes that haven't been recognized and consciously cultivated. There are, of course, some potentials we should not act out, but it is better if our actions are governed by self-aware choices and not unconscious repressions.

The more unconscious we are, the less real knowledge of ourselves we have, the more projecting we do, and the more we lose ourselves to the people and the world around us. This problem, caused by our lack of self-awareness, brings us face-to-face with another predicament. Separating our inner images of the feminine and archetypal feminine from real women is, in reality, an almost lifelong task in the pursuit of self-knowledge. The image that we have developed and internalized from our experience of our mother is to a large extent the source of all of our feminine images. Our first image of the feminine comes from our early perception of our mother and our experiences of her. This image dwells on some level of our unconscious from that point on. Throughout our lives, the women in our personal world affect the development of who we are as women or the development of the inner feminine in men and, in both of these cases, influence how we think of and deal with women in the larger world. As a consequence, we find today that the wound to the feminine and the split between empowering women's animus while culturally denigrating the feminine principle has left many women and men not trusting women and each other. We have only touched on this split, but we will develop this idea further as we proceed.

Effects of the Evil Eye

In folklore, the Gorgon Medusa was regarded as a symbol of casting an evil eye. In this context, the evil eye was defined as a glance that had the power to cast a malignant spell, bringing bad luck, illness, or death. The evil eye could be avoided by capturing its reflection in a mirror, and the reflection could then be turned against an enemy. For this very reason, we find the image of Medusa on ancient shields, tombs, vases, coins, and ovens used by bakers or potters, wherever human efforts were uncertain and danger might be lurking. Even in ancient times, the myth and image of Medusa had begun to serve helpful and redemptive purposes. In order to ward off evil, the Gorgon face functioned at once to mirror the face of the evil one and to cast back at it just as evil a stare.

Casting an evil spell is actually a very good analogy for what we do when we make a projection, and damaging projections are made worldwide. There are many examples of our defenses against evil projections, including the use of an intense stare, amulets, phallic gestures of the hand to assert life over death, or sticking out the tongue in derision or anger. Even the veil of the bride serves to ward off envy. Phrases like "break a leg" before any kind of performance—or in Italy "in bocca al lupo," which means "in the mouth of the wolf"—are still used whenever we face challenges of some sort.

These are a few examples from folklore of the psychology of shadow projections. In these examples, the evil eye points to the shadowy parts of ourselves that we would prefer not to know or even be aware of. These are aspects of ourselves that we want to deny and that, therefore, often get projected. Folklore treats these situations very seriously. This tradition enables us to see that our projections, especially our negative ones, are not harmless. Frequently, they inflict a moral injury: They disturb the well-being of the person making the projections, and they significantly affect the person onto whom the projection falls. We all know that a negative projection from a respected, feared, or important person in our lives can immobilize us, make us unable to feel or think well, or even make us unable to work. In these kinds of projections, we find the sting of Medusa and the fangs of her snakes.

Discussing projections brings to mind a situation I observed some years ago. I remember a particular priest who was very polished at being quietly sarcastic as he developed caricatures of certain people in his parish. His facial expressions added dry wit to his humor, and he could make people roar with laughter. But his humor also had a darker side. In one case, he often made allusions to a particular woman who, he thought, was stuck-up and had been raised by a wealthy family in Charleston, South Carolina. In his eyes, she never had to work because she always had maids doing everything for her. When she volunteered her free time for the church, he assigned her jobs that nobody else wanted to do, like cleaning the silver or the vestry. She grumbled but carried out her duties for many years while the priest continued to amuse people with his humorous satires. Then he moved to another church and everyone lost touch with him. Years later, I saw an obituary and the photograph looked familiar. The obituary turned out to be for the same woman who had been doing the tedious jobs at the church for all those years. In the obituary, there was a brief account of her life. I discovered that she had not been raised in Charleston and that she had lost her father at a young age. In reality, she had been raised in a small town by her single mother, and they had endured huge financial difficulties. The projection of this priest limited this woman's giving heart, her generosity, and some of her potential for spiritual growth. They also prevented him from really knowing her as a person and lessened the sense of community for both of them.

Even though sarcasm can seem very funny, it can be a clever way of delivering, in a symbolic knapsack, the venomous head of Medusa in the form of projected evil. A lively social gathering can provide the safeguard for those who use sarcasm. In such settings we cannot defend ourselves from their attacks because we would be accused of lacking a sense of humor or taking life too seriously. But deep inside, we know we have been diminished. This energy is unpleasant and difficult when it comes from acquaintances, but it is most destructive when it comes from someone close to us, whom we are supposed to love and respect—and who is supposed to love us—such as a mother or father.

Projections and Reality

We have all experienced the destructive effects of the projections onto the feminine in Western societies. These projections trace their origins to the joining of the patriarchy with institutionalized monotheism. The patriarchy grew out of the middle ages into the Age of Reason, and this movement birthed a cultural mentality that became rational, verbal, and literal. This new mindset rejected the mythological and symbolic values in our religious writings, which had nurtured and guided people's lives for centuries. Today, because we have lost these values and are allowing information to replace knowledge, we no longer realize that symbols and images carry a deeper reality than words. Part of our devaluation of the feminine results from our loss of the art of thinking symbolically. To lose this art is to lose the kind of grounding that enables us to experience the beautiful depths of love and the Divine presence that is potentially within our capacities.

Let us enlarge our focus on the myth of Medusa. As we do so, we can imagine that as Zeus emerged as the ruler on Mount Olympus, he represented the developing image of the will to organize and control life and of power based on the authority of the intellect. Zeus ruled from a detached place, on high, and his creation of order and structure brought with it a fear of change and of threats to the status quo. In Zeus, we have the beginning of a dominant principle in the psyche of Western history.

Let us consider Poseidon, the brother of Zeus, as well. Poseidon represents the origins of another dominant principle in the Western psyche. Generally more severe and rough than Zeus, he is the god of the sea and its storms and of earthquakes. But in his early mythological development, he began as a fertility god, a god of the earth who sent up springs to nourish life. Then as his power grew, the nature of his

73

character seemed to become more tempestuous and dominating. Poseidon became a symbol of superiority and dominance over nature, and perhaps a forebear of our preoccupation with dominating the natural, material world.

Western monotheism continued in this same vein as it introduced the notion of spiritual superiority over the natural world. In very general terms, when this tradition is taken literally and its stories are not seen symbolically, it, too, becomes a principle of dominance, spiritual dominance. In this construct, spiritual superiority comes from the subjugation of our human nature as well as nature in general, which includes the feminine and our sexuality.

If we combine our two relatively unconscious but dominant principles, we are led into believing, at an unconscious level, that we can or should be able to control life. We also start to develop the illusion that we can be, or it is preferable to be, detached and above life intellectually, spiritually, and emotionally. The results of these patriarchal complexes in our cultural and, therefore, personal unconscious cause us to think we can carry out our goals, translate our ideas and designs into actions, and change our attitudes at will. When we do not succeed in these endeavors, we then label ourselves as being lazy, weak, undisciplined, or inadequate or simply as failures. Not only is this a one-sided, patriarchal approach to life, but it is also a very damaging approach. Jung says clearly in *Man and His Symbols* (p. 82) that such an orientation requires us to pay a price based on "a remarkable lack of introspection." He continues by saying that we are blind to the fact that with all of our rationality and efficiency, we are possessed by "powers" that are beyond our control. And the price we pay for our illusions is that these powers keep us "on the run with restlessness, vague apprehensions, psychological complications, an insatiable need for pills, alcohol, tobacco, food—and above all, a large array of neuroses."

There is a further element to consider. This one-sided approach to life leads us to the mistaken idea that we can rationally choose our goals, single out and change our attitudes, organize and implement our lives efficiently, trusting that these abilities should guide us to healthy self-esteem, success, and a good life. But following this path actually means we would prefer a good life as defined by our patriarchal/marketing society, including our self-help marketing society, and in compensation to our early wounds and complexes. In this way, we set ourselves up to experience continuous cycles of shame simply because we cannot meet the expectations that we have created, because they are based on these illusions.

As analysts, one of the hardest things that we have to do is help people overcome their hidden contempt for the feminine as they begin their inner work. People in our society are easily swallowed up by busyness, productivity, and their crammed schedules. The modern technology that promised easy free time has brought, instead, tension, anxiety, and a compulsion to get more of the same. To escape this cycle, we have to learn to sacrifice some of the values and activities in this driven approach. This entails giving new appreciation and respect to taking time for silence and reflection as well as being receptive to and nurturing our inner lives. This necessity is as urgent for men as it is for women, and it lies in the heart of the archetypal feminine: relatedness, receptivity, and valuing the non-rational. Until we make this shift in how we value ourselves and life, our ability to respond with intense interest and love to each other and to ideas will be fettered. Our deepest creativity needs a transformed atmosphere in which to flourish.

We need to pause for a moment in order to see how the effects of these negative projections on the feminine are crippling. They are generated by our patriarchal complexes (e.g., we are not really doing anything, we are wasting time, etc.) onto things that are not oriented toward achievement or "doing what has to be done" and also limit our ability to experience our emotions. To be more "efficient," we are supposed to be detached from our emotions, above them and in control of them. The truth of the matter is that by adopting this perspective, we are beating down what should be handled with care. When we repress our emotions, we create their counterparts in our unconscious, where, without the light of consciousness, the will becomes dark, explosive, destructive, and increasingly overwhelming in some way. Our emotions are the only way we can be personally engaged in life. Having the strength to experience our emotions, without being overwhelmed by them, and being able to learn from them are the keys to a psychologically healthy life. On the other hand, if we avoid knowing our psychological and emotional needs, as the projections from our patriarchal complexes compel us to do, we feel isolated. We can easily see that when we have such a hidden contempt for the feminine and when we live lives of over-rationality, over-control of our emotions, efficiency, and productivity, we are feeding the Death Mother complex. When we deny our engagement in life—the warmth of our emotions and even the heat of them—and see them negatively, the Death Mother takes this rejected energy and uses it to invade our world and our deep inner selves with a cold, fierce, corrosive power that kills hope and drains our vitality.

Before we continue our focus on projections, let's examine a further point that is inherent in the patriarchy. The patriarchy, and the internalized patriarchal complex in men and women, lives in fear of having the status quo threatened. This, too, is part of the negative projection on the feminine's ability to stir up change and transformation. It is also one of the main reasons we dread our emotions: Because if we really perceive and understand our emotions, we may have to face the daunting task of changing our lives. Collectively and individually, we fear the transformative nature of the feminine. We view challenges to the institutional status quo of society—and, even more important, challenges to the way we have "institutionalized" our lives, feelings, value systems, and expectations—with dismay. Those of us who shun the transformational aspects of the feminine have projected our fears of our feminine nature (which include our fears of confronting our lives, traditions, attitudes, and history) onto the images of women that range from Eve, to witches, to bitches, to gold diggers, to hysterics.

Let's consider the story of Eve and the snake, which has been used to denigrate women for centuries. The biblical tradition of this story, as it is interpreted in a literal and shallow way, is that nature as we know it, especially human nature, is corrupt, and woman as temptress is a corrupter of men and social values. I believe that anyone who thinks this tradition has not affected women at a deep level or the way men fear the feminine within themselves hasn't been paying attention to how we feel about ourselves. When Bud has answered questions about this story during his lectures on mysticism, he refers to it as the story of our fall out of naïve unconsciousness and into the opposites that define the struggles and potentials of life. By reflecting on the opposites of life and death, sickness and health, joy and sorrow, consciousness and unconsciousness, we learn that growth results from repeating processes of transformation, life, death, and rebirth experiences. We must struggle for a life of consciousness, and this consciousness, when gained, increases our capacity for love and for experiencing the Divine. Eve and the serpent can be regarded as symbols of the feminine and its transformational aspects. We all know that in mythology, the image of woman symbolizes life. From this perspective, we can imagine that the violation of Medusa, a mortal woman in the myth, is a violation of life. And when we let a power principle violate life, it turns a nasty face toward us.

According to Joseph Campbell in *The Power of Myth* (p. 47), "Woman brings life into the world. Eve is the mother of the temporal world." The archetypal feminine is the mother of how we experience life, just as our collective unconscious is the mother of our consciousness from the standpoint of Jungian psychology. If we literalize the story of Adam and Eve, we lose its great lessons and meaning. Perhaps we should be learning from it that life is a struggle for our development of wholeness. I believe one lesson here is that we need to learn enough about love, mercy, and compassion to realize sickness and death are meant to teach us that life is precious; these experiences are bumps in our road that can ultimately make our lives more profound, meaningful, and bearable. If we keep searching for the Garden of Eden of happiness, we stop looking for meaning and transformation. We throw our lives away and allow others to do the same, like tossing McDonald's wrappers out of a car window. This is not the way of the archetypal feminine, of love, of Eros—or even of the Great Mother, who is the mother of life, of transformation, and of death. Let us learn the deeper messages from Eve and not be so quick to embrace the projections that rob our religious and mythological stories of their meaning.

The Other Side of Projections

Another essential observation about projections is that frequently what we project is not a negative characteristic that we despise but, rather, a positive quality. Each of us possesses positive values within our shadow that, for whatever reasons, we haven't been able to own. Consequently, we search for these qualities and project them onto things outside of ourselves. Jung wrote that our idea that God is love is partially a projection. By this he meant that we unconsciously project onto the Divine the highest value that we have been unable to actualize but would like to live by.

Once we become aware that we do project, we have to ask ourselves, why does this projection come out of me? The reason is that a projection is a defense mechanism. An individual's need for such a defense mechanism results from the deep experiences of life and the needs for healing and wholeness within the Self. Projections are structured by the Self and by individual needs. So, as an example, we might ask, what did the priest need to develop or face in himself that he was projecting onto the woman he was ridiculing? Perhaps he needed to confront his own mother complex; his own arrogance; or his fear of his anima, of the feminine, or of women in general. By facing his projection, taking it back, working to understand and integrate it, what could he have learned about himself? The priest missed the opportunity to see how he could have broadened himself and become more fully human.

Just as an individual's projection can reveal a deep wound, the common projections we share with others show our collective need for healing and transformation. The interest that so many women have shared in exploring the meaning of mythological and divine feminine figures—the goddess, the Madonna, the Black Madonna, Quan Yin, the crone, and Athena—indicates that deep inside we are compelled to seek and develop our experiences and understanding of the archetypal feminine and to integrate it into our lives. The Death Mother stands against this quest and masks it as a waste of time. So, we must enter this conflict with a love of life, seeking transformation and the understanding we need to confront and heal this complex.

The Fear of Transformation

One of the most puzzling problems analysts face is why people hold on to their unhappy lives or even the hell they are living in, with all of its frustrations and pain, rather than seek to change. The problem, I think, is that choosing the inner journey into self-knowledge and wholeness entails (1) a commitment to the value of *our* life and (2) the suffering that necessarily comes from this course, even though that suffering is healing and redemptive. The unhappiness and hell that we might be living can usually be rationalized onto circumstances, fate, family, or some other source; though in reality, we may be the source of it. Jung said that most of our suffering is neurotic suffering, and it comes from our inability or unwillingness to face ourselves, make the needed commitments to change, and endure the suffering of our process of transformation.

We are all indoctrinated into the social character of our culture. The social character of our culture—the sea we all swim in, so to speak—sees material happiness as our goal. It has a limited perception of our abilities to make ourselves deep, value life, love in more profound ways, heal ourselves, and live into our life's potential, which is beyond our everyday vision. Our social character sells humanity short, and so do our conventional medical, psychological, and even religious communities. The path we are talking about in this book will require commitment, suffering, and energy. It will also enable us to discover our core wounds—and our core loves and potentials to live in new, more enriching ways.

People sometimes ask me, "Why do I have to go back into all this old stuff? Can't you just help me get on with my life?" My answer to those questions is no. The experiences that make up our early lives are the foundations of who we are, and they are patterned in our brains to be repeated and to control us, until we heal them. Healing begins with restoring those parts of ourselves that have been scattered, hidden, suppressed, denied, distorted, and forbidden. It begins, especially, with restoring our ability to cultivate our emotions and our willingness to ask life for things for ourselves. Developing self-knowledge is more than gathering information about ourselves. One of its most important aspects is to re-member: to bring together the parts and integrate what pain has alienated us from, what fear has separated us from, and what our need for safety has caused us to disdain. Our inner journey into self-knowledge begins with re-membering, restoring, revitalizing, rescuing, reclaiming, and renewing. Myths like the one we are exploring help us structure our re-membering.

The very process of this mythic journey transforms us as we live it and our old self breaks down so that a new one may emerge, like a phoenix from the ashes. We are also transforming our history into a history that will support our becoming. In her paper "The Structural Forms of the Feminine Psyche" (p. 5), the Jungian analyst Toni Wolff writes that the transformational aspect of the Great Mother archetype instinctually "protects the process of becoming, of what is undeveloped, in need of protection, in danger, or must be tended, cared for and assisted." In this journey, our nature will support us, and we must learn to take a loftier view of our possibilities than we have been encouraged to take.

Chapter 6

THE REALITY OF MEDUSA'S MYTH

When the soul wishes to experience something, she throws an image of the experience out before her and enters into her own image.

— MEISTER ECKHART

Myths reflect the archetypal patterns in our psyche that structure our experiences of living. These patterns are something like a riverbed that the flow of water, human experience, has created over time. These mythic patterns support and channel our lives. If we can begin to live with some awareness of our mythic patterns, we find that they can help us redeem our lives and assist us along the way as we encounter shoals and rapids, difficulties and the unexpected. Mythic stories are especially helpful when we are suffering, though living the myths will bring us face-to-face with life's darkness—especially the life, death, and renewal aspects of transformation—before they lead us into healing and help us become whole. But we can be comforted as we remember that there is no journey without a myth, and there is no journey, no healing, no transformation in life without suffering.

As we consider the myth of Medusa, if we are bold enough to read it slowly and let it sink into our emotions and our imagination, we will observe a constant stream of power. This power will touch the recesses of our hearts and push into the shadowy corners of our soul, into places we didn't know were there. If we are able to wonder about how it must have felt for Medusa to be so beautiful and so naïve, and then to think about how violently she was treated by Poseidon and Athena, we may remember moments in our lives when tender feelings were crushed and our trusting hearts were violated. Medusa was forced from a vital existence into passivity and hiding. In imagining our own early experiences, it is helpful to ask ourselves if we or parts of us were forced into a similar hidden stance. Then we can ask ourselves what choices we had to make. Did we have to choose achievement to get affirmation? Or did we have to choose to put our parents and others first in our efforts to feel safe? Or did we become stuck in other endless efforts for safety, recognition, or approval that caused us to lose our grip on our own development?

Speaking for myself, I came to realize that the variations, struggles, and details in my personal life formed a journey that was just as dramatic, at times just as traumatic, and at other times just as heroic as the story that unfolds in the myth of Medusa. As a woman in Italy, which is like in most places in the Western world, I had to seek my identity and self-respect in a masculine world—one of accomplishments, ideas, and opinions, especially those of others. In this process, part of me was brutalized and banished: the deep feminine part. Much later, I had to confront this part of myself and help it become transformed through the death of my own woundedness and the rebirth of a different kind of healing power and vitality, like the healing power that came from Medusa's blood.

I was shocked when, after I had studied and known the story of Athena for many years, I came to the realization that she had not been mothered. I knew the story of Metis, who had been made pregnant by Zeus. It was predicted that she would give birth to a child who was destined to become greater than him. To avert the prophecy's fulfillment, Zeus swallowed Metis, and at the end of nine months, Athena sprang fully armored from his head. It seems obvious, but it took me a long time to figure it out. Athena had never been mothered. Neither had I. But I didn't realize this reality in a flash of insight. I did years of heartbreaking inner work before I could accept that I had never been mothered in the emotional sense or loved simply because I was there.

I remember how my family ridiculed me with biting sarcasm because of my interest in books, languages, and art. Looking back, I realized I must have felt like Athena competing for the golden apple against Hera, the goddess of being a wife and homemaker, and Aphrodite, the goddess of love. My family's judgment was like the judgment of Paris. No one in my family seriously considered that a woman could be intelligent, powerful, forthright, and also lovable, desirable, and sensual. So, like Athena, I armored myself against ridicule and my loneliness and sent a deep, inner feminine part of myself into an inner cavern.

Athena plays a crucial role in Medusa's myth: She represents how our culture has helped create the Death Mother. It is also interesting to note that Athena helps Perseus redeem this situation. And, as I have also worked with men as an analyst for decades, I have seen firsthand how important the development of the feminine is to us all and how this process must be respected in order for men to unfold their inner feminine capacities.

In chapter 1, I explained that many of us are born psychologically without ever really coming into the light. Now, once again, we can ask ourselves, what does this metaphor mean? I believe it means that even before we came out of the womb, many of us were carrying on our back, as I illustrated with the image of the remora, our mother's emotional makeup—her fear, her anxiety, her anger, her despair, and her feelings of being overwhelmed, of not being safe and supported, and of not being sufficiently valued by her family and culture. We must also keep in mind that mothers like Timothy's mother, who was affluent and socially active, or Erin's mother, who was a successful business-woman, or my own mother, who was the picture of a good wife, may seem happy and engaged. Yet, deep beneath the surface of their lives, a vital feminine part of themselves has been banished and become withdrawn, frozen, and bitter.

The picture of the remora, the large fish attached to the man's back, is a good reminder that we carry this Death Mother complex—this Medusa complex that drains our energy, saps our vitality, and drags us down. This complex will often cause us to live emotionally and creatively limited lives and to freeze when initiative is called for. I must repeat that this complex, the most draining complex we face today, strikes at the foundation of our entire personality, and for this reason, we have a crucial and urgent need to confront it. I use such dramatic terms because I have experienced how much the Death Mother complex has affected my whole life, my husband's life, the lives of my stepchildren, and the lives of the men and women I have worked with professionally.

Throughout my work with this complex, I have discovered that using the myth of Medusa—sitting in the mythic reality of our inner worlds, where we can experience its underlying truth and power—can give us a roadmap for transformation. Then our Death Mother complex can move from being very destructive to fostering a new level of energy that we never dreamed we had.

The Moment of Impact

I'm sure that you will remember that Medusa did not start out as an ugly monster or as an immortal. She had grown into a beautiful woman who unfortunately caught the eye of the great sea god, Poseidon, the brother of Zeus. Poseidon raped her in the temple of the goddess Athena. This act of desecration enraged Athena who, as we have seen, was identified with the patriarchal gods and who was jealous of Medusa's beauty. How quick we are to be like Athena and identify with values that are active, productive, dynamic, sports-oriented, achievement-oriented, practical, clear, structured, and linear. Then, like Athena, we become both angry at and envious of the different and impractical values of slowness, waiting, stillness, contemplating, yielding, receiving, the hidden, the secret, and the absorbing. These are the values and nurturance, the beauty of the feminine in human life. This side of life is imperiled when Medusa, the symbol of the beauty in human life, is ravished by the power principle and is punished by Athena, who supports patriarchal values.

We have, of course, benefited from how we have structured our society and used science and technology. Our greatest concern is to guard against incorporating, as we are actually doing, the mechanical, power-oriented aspects of the patriarchy and against losing ourselves as we try to find our identity, as defined by our society's values.

We can imagine the double pain that Medusa must have felt, to be raped and then to have Athena punish her for being the victim by turning her beautiful hair into a nest of snakes and making her beautiful face so terrible to look at that it turned whoever saw it into stone. We, too, are faced with a double wounding: The social character of our society supports an identity based on the patriarchal values I have described, which at a certain point can alienate us from who we really are and can become. Further, we are wounded most severely through our parents, especially our mothers, who should be the carriers of love, nurturance, and safety and not the remora of the Death Mother complex.

Once Medusa had been so horribly transformed, she was banished, or what we might call repressed deeply into the unconscious. There, living in a cave, she was still very powerful and turned many people and animals into stone. This power represents how she could, symbolizing a wound or a complex, paralyze our potentials and instinctual lives. When we have such a dominant complex in our unconscious, it controls our lives. No matter what we tell ourselves, no matter how aggressive, in control or even positive we appear, we are unable to make real choices about our lives until we have healed and transformed this complex. Until we have begun that process, the major themes, choices, and actions in our lives will be driven either by the complex, which includes our unhealed woundedness, or by our reaction to it.

Perseus and the Quest for Transformation

Every myth represents a treasure-house of wisdom regarding the world and our personality. On the other hand, the way to these treasures is difficult and tangled. All too often when it seems like the mythic map is clear, we suddenly discover that there is a whole new level of the myth before us. Myths are meant to take us beyond ourselves, beyond the ways we have looked at life and particularly at our difficulties and struggles. For example in *The Odyssey*, we find two levels in the story.

The first is the quest of Telemachus to find his father. The second is the quest of Odysseus to return home to his wife. In mythic terms, Telemachus is searching for his own inner authority and Odysseus is trying to return home through a journey haunted by his encounters with feminine figures. Both quests come together as Odysseus completes the symbolic masculine search for the inner feminine. Myths are about the realization of different aspects of our wholeness, and they are not about gender roles. They reflect how the archetypal patterns of the masculine and feminine live and intertwine in all of us. And they describe what happens when such patterns become one-sided: Nature sets the stage to redirect them through journeys of transformation.

When the feminine and our vitality become lost to power drives and life becomes a wasteland, the stage is set for the mythic world to give rise to a hero to transform and revitalize the situation. The mythic hero is a metaphor for our struggle to transform our consciousness and bring new life to ourselves. The reality is that we experience the difficulties of the situation these myths depict. We experience the wounding of Medusa as part of ourselves, and we experience the helplessness of Perseus's mother, Danaë—the feminine in the land of a patriarchal king or, psychologically, a patriarchal ruling principle in our psyche and culture. But within us is the drive to transform this situation toward healing and wholeness. We know this drive is there because the myth is an archetypal expression of it. It is as if the desire for transformation is part of our psychic DNA. Our quest is to become conscious of it and to cooperate with it. In this process, we will find the archetypal energies of the masculine and feminine being brought forth for transformation, working with each other. Simply put, when we turn within to seek self-knowledge, healing, and growth, these inner forces will be there to support us.

Once Medusa is banished, the myth continues by picking up the second story, that of the emergence of Perseus as the hero that will transform the now repressed and poisonous energy of Medusa. We find that as Perseus was entering manhood, he lived without a father, which is a situation we find in many of the myths about heroes. I mentioned before that on an archetypal level, such a son carries the image of his mother's inner quest and its symbolic psychological pattern. The myth's plot thickens when King Polydectes decides that he wants to marry Perseus's mother. This situation suggests the problem that we have when an old ruling principle in our psyche or culture, such as old patriarchal principles that are trying to control the feminine within us or life, is being threatened by a new principle, the hero.

Perseus in his youth and naïveté wanted to please this old principle, as many of us do when we try too hard to please our parents, over-perform in school, or deny our own reality and needs in our efforts to gain acceptance, approval, or even safety. We should note that Perseus and his mother were living at the largesse of the king. Because of his desire to please the king and protect his mother, Perseus rashly consented to pursue the impossible task of getting the head of Medusa for the king.

The complexities of meanings and the intricacies of the patterns' interactions in the myth bring to mind the complexities of ourselves and how we grow and transform. As we examine each image in the myth, we see that every masculine image also has a connection to a feminine one and every feminine image has connections to masculine ones. Each has a connection to some part of both the masculine and feminine principles. Perseus, as a growing symbol of the masculine, has a connection to the mother, Danaë, who, as a symbol of the feminine and the mother, is connected to her son, Perseus. For centuries, these mythic images have reflected both the masculine and feminine principles on different levels. The deeper we go in one, the closer we are to the other—which can enhance, destroy, or transform us. Symbolically, we see an illustration that the masculine and feminine, like the Yang and Yin, constantly combine and interact. They grow together and enhance each other's progress if we hold them in consciousness, in perspective, seeking full awareness of both. If we fall short in our awareness, however, their interaction can become destructive and even deadly. The myths of the Greeks show that tragedies are the result of our failure to be consciously aware of what is going on in our lives. Fortunately for Perseus, Athena, who was also the patron goddess of heroes, and the god Hermes helped him in his quest by giving him a proper strategy and the arms he needed.

Perseus Begins His Journey

Once Perseus had received the help of Athena and Hermes, he also needed the help of the nymphs, whom he could locate only by consulting the Graeae, the old ones. As Perseus's journey began, his encounters, except for his meeting with Hermes, related to the feminine. After leaving his mother in preparation for his journey, he was helped by the unmothered Athena. Athena sent him to the Graeae in order to find the nymphs, and as he began his quest, he underwent a series of encounters with the feminine as a rite of preparation for facing Medusa. The myth is showing us that as we initiate this inner journey, we must begin confronting ourselves a step at a time. We must build up both the courage and our ability to confront ourselves. This approach is necessary because all too often, we are starting from a place where our real knowledge of ourselves has been forbidden, where we have been living in exile outside of ourselves and in a society that doesn't value inner experience.

The Graeae, three old women who share a single eye and a single tooth, are showing us old points of view: the narrow perspective of the status quo in society. Perseus must steal their eye—their mental outlook—and use this theft to trick them, in order to find out where the nymphs are. We can remain at this low level of consciousness, symbolized by the Graeae, and live with a false sense of security. Or, like Perseus, we can confront the values we have grown accustomed to in our society and our families, but without totally destroying them, so we can find our way to the nymphs that are the feminine in nature.

The Graeae are a good illustration of where we find ourselves when we give up and go with the flow of our families and culture. We may feel secure, but in reality, we are trapped in a state of mind and awareness that are below our potentials. This is a tedious position without vitality, without creativity, in a place that does not cultivate love, imagination, and individuality. Our cultural perspective or so-called conventional wisdom, for example, is generally a one-sided point of view based on scarcity and fear. The fear it engenders can be the fear of ridicule, disapproval, or rejection or being thought of as selfish, weird, or just not right.

The Graeae, which in Greek means the "gray ones," "old women," or "gray sisters," never lived their youth. Consequently, when we identify with them, we lose our perspective, our capacity for growth. All too often, we give up and choose a life of safety in the status quo, denying our hunger for adventure and growth. We forget audacity and courage and settle for a false sense of security and timidity. Some of us spend our entire lives in this psychological state of mind and become trapped in this condition of sleepwalking through life.

If we experience the Death Mother while we are growing up, we will internalize this negative archetypal energy. In the course of time, it will become written in our physical bodies, as it was reflected in the bodies of the Graeae. They were said, in some versions of the myth, to have the distorted bodies of swans. What could have been naturally beautiful was now distorted and ugly. If while growing up we had the sense of being unacceptable to our parents, being resented or not wanted by them, or being threatened by them, our nervous system will become hypervigilant and our ego, the center of who we believe we are, will become withdrawn and defensive. As soon as we experience a breath of rejection or ridicule, we will close down and become blind and helpless, paralyzed. We will find ourselves automatically, no matter how much we hate it, repeating the survival mechanism we used while growing up, and we may stay absolutely still, withdrawn, and detached in order, we unconsciously hope, not to attract attention.

As our hopelessness grows, these patterns may evolve into defensive mechanisms that are also physical, such as vomiting, being overweight, migraines, and other symptoms. Such symptoms are an effort to keep the poison out and to avoid dealing with our core inner issue. What often adds insult to injury in these situations is that our medical profession makes us, especially women, feel ridiculed by implying, if not outright saying, that it is "all in our heads" or that our problems are genetic. And in either case, we are supposed to take a pill. From Jungian psychology, we know that frequently these symptoms result from a complex that has been internalized—and sometimes from a complex that has been handed down for generations. Complexes easily go from one generation to the next until someone gets desperate enough or conscious enough to do the inner work needed to bring this problem into consciousness and then transform it.

In my family, my mother had frequent digestive problems and eventually had to have major surgery. All of her five children also have or had digestive problems as well. My two sisters had major surgeries on their stomachs. Growing up, I vomited on a regular basis, and these problems eventually came to an end after I entered analysis. Early in my work on this topic, I had the following dream.

I was in the large hallway of my childhood home, with the marble floor shining beautifully. On the floor were two carrying boxes with my present cats inside of them. I experienced a very tender feeling for them. Next to the boxes was a big pile of dirt that went surprisingly deep into the ground. A black cord of some type was on the top of the pile. I grasped it firmly and began pulling it. It seemed to be very long and coming from deep within the earth because I pulled at it for a long time. As I was pulling, the cord got larger, and I realized that I was now pulling a python, which was very angry. Then he was totally out of his hole and hissing at me, in a position to attack.

I woke from this dream scared and exhausted. For the next three days, I had a terrible stomachache and I had to stay in bed, just like when I was growing up. At the end of those three days, I felt like discussing this dream with my husband. While I was sharing with him the associations that the dream stirred up in me, I was able to put into words my emotions and heartaches from long ago, as if a doorway had opened into my emotional past. As I finished sharing some of my deepest of feelings and understandings, I experienced a long gurgle in my stomach, like the ground settling in the deepest reaches of my internal organs. Instantly, I had the clear perception that I was healed, as if the primordial beast in my stomach that had made me so miserable were now gone.

On a symbolic level, I also felt reassured that this dream was now telling me that I have the necessary strength to slowly, hand over hand, pull this complex out of the unconscious and bring it into conscious awareness. Once I was conscious of the complex, I could face it and relate to it. In that process, we would transform each other. Reflecting on this dream, I could be confident that my unconscious was supporting me. My engagement with this dream was an important turning point that urged me to work more energetically and hopefully on this intimidating material.

This turning point became the place in my inner work where I could reach into myself to a greater extent and—when I was ready to finally begin to connect with my true energy and vitality—the place where I could find the valiant Perseus within me. The mythic pattern, the archetypal pattern within us, promises us that if we pursue this inner journey with all of our hearts, these turning points will come. Our unconscious will support us.

We may also think of Perseus as representing the first stage of development in a woman's animus, her masculine side. During this stage, a woman develops the internal strength that needs to be freed and cultivated in order for her to form her own voice and identity. For a man, we may think of Perseus as representing the masculine ego strength he needs in order to consolidate his identity and to separate from the dominating negativity of his mother complex. This separation is necessary for a man—even for one who thinks he has a positive mother complex, because even a "positive" complex affects us negatively. Any complex that is active in our personality has the capacity to take us over, keep us in the grip of its behaviors and emotions, and color our perceptions of ourselves, others, and life in ways that we have no control over. The Perseus image represents our developing inner strength, as the myth of Medusa shows us how to slay the Death Mother complex, thereby transforming its energies and freeing our own feelings of empowerment. And in this way, identity and voice develop.

The reality of the myth of Medusa is so harsh that many people have difficulty accepting it. In other words, we are loath to initially admit that an injury so unjust and so terrible has been inflicted on us. The well-known child psychologist Alice Miller, in her book *The Body Never Lies: The Lingering Effects of Hurtful Parenting*, writes that we all live under the harmful effects of the fourth commandment in the Old

Testament. This commandment, which tells us to honor our parents, has become so entrenched in our cultural unconscious that it thwarts our ability to heal early injuries. Unless there is literal sexual and physical abuse—and sometimes even then—far too many people in the "caring professions" side with this injunction, rather than recognizing the consequences of many early injuries. The power of this point of view not only keeps us from realizing the truth of our own experiences but also subtly causes us to blame ourselves for the destructive parenting we received. It sets us on a compulsive path of self-deception: We deny our injuries and the truth of our own reality, not to mention the reality of our emotional experience.

All too often we repress the reality of our early lives into a deep cave in our psyche. For example, for many years I said, and I thought, that I had a wonderful mother and a happy childhood. I also thought that my family was superior to many others and that we were just better morally and materially. But as I examined myself more intensely during my analysis in Zurich, I learned that life is not so simple. After entering analysis, my viewpoint changed dramatically. Piece by piece, this illusion of mine broke apart.

If we cannot "see" the Medusa in our life, it very likely means that we are keeping a good persona intact for our own comfort or that we are caught in a cycle of inner struggle that is blinding us to the real complex driving us. I will say more about this cycle later. If we are protecting our persona and the comfortable way we view ourselves, then we are probably projecting our Death Mother complex as a shadow or negative anima figure onto other people, such as lovers, bosses, spouses, the government, churches, and other such institutions. These projections are powerful and they make us feel better about ourselves. They may even give us a sense of superiority and righteousness.

As we finish this chapter, it will be helpful if you reflect on a few of the things we have discussed. Do these reflections in your journal, with a pencil and paper, on your computer, or however is most comfortable for you. Quietly ask yourself the following questions, and then give yourself four or five minutes to write your responses to each one, describing the feelings, images, and thoughts that come up in you.

92

1. How conscious am I of how the Medusa in my life affects me?
2. What kinds of emotions do these thoughts bring up in me? Where do I feel them in my body?
3. How have I projected the Medusa outside of me?
4. What central theme dominates the fable about my childhood that I made up to protect myself?
5. What do I project onto a man or woman who is taking the time to be quiet, to be still, to be passive, to be receptive, or to be contemplative? How do I discriminate between these states of being and those valued by our patriarchal culture, such as being active, productive, and dynamic? Do I project different things onto a man and a woman who are behaving in the same way?
6. What other points or questions in this chapter do I think are important for me to explore?

PART THREE

Burning Clean

If we arrange our life according to that principle which counsels us that we must always hold to the difficult, then that which now still seems to us the most alien will become what we most trust and find most faithful.

— RAINER MARIA RILKE

Chapter 7

WOMEN TURNED TO STONE— CONFRONTING FEAR

Fear is a question: What are you afraid of and why? Just as the seed of health is in illness, because illness contains information, our fears are a treasure house of self-knowledge if we explore them.

– MARILYN FERGUSON

Throughout this book, we have seen that when we encounter the Medusa deep inside of us, we become paralyzed by her gaze, paralyzed by fear. But in the myth, we see that Perseus becomes paralyzed, in effect, even before he gets anywhere close to Medusa and her cave. Once he had committed himself to the quest to kill Medusa, he ended up wandering in the wilds, overwhelmed by the task he had set up for himself and lost in fear. We, too, face this initial fear that is close to paralyzing, is confusing, and, more often than not, leaves us feeling hopeless.

If we look at Perseus from a psychological point of view, we could say that he had a traumatic childhood. There was no father; he and his mother were cast out of their secure home, abandoned, and endured a perilous voyage. With time, they found some degree of protection and shelter. But their security was never permanent, as Perseus discovered when he ended up having to face his journey to kill Medusa. These circumstances remind me that even in difficult circumstances, our psyche tries to protect us during our early years and to give us little islands of inner sanctity and security. They may be islands of fantasy, introversion, imaginary lands or stories to live in, imaginary friends, imaginary parents, a nurturing grandparent, or religious images. But whatever this world is, as we mature in adulthood, if we are to heal and become who we have the potential to become, we must leave this world behind and begin the quest to face the Death Mother and her power, which negates our source of life and vitality.

Perseus's commitment to the quest has brought him face-to-face with a *developmental paradox* that we all have to face, and initially, it is a very unpleasant situation to face and accept. This paradox is that growing from one stage to another, from one state of being to another, is a process that involves loss, perceived dangers, risks, and some degree of suffering. And our culture is no help to us at all, because it vigorously denies this reality, which we all have to confront. Our society promotes the idea that childhood should be a happy and carefree time. It is anything but that. It should be a time of nurturance, security, and safety. Yet childhood must also be a time of risk, fear, discovery, failure, and accomplishment of developmental necessities.

From the beginning, we have to face the reality that any new personal development, especially in terms of our personality and maturing potentials, means giving up the security of our present position. We must take risks and encounter danger, fear, and even suffering. For this reason, we need our parents—and ideally our society as well—to provide a cushion of love and security for us to fall back on, to serve as a foundation for our continued growth. We don't get to make a lot of choices about what happens to us in our early life and its situations. Most of us can identify with the risks of starting kindergarten, changing schools, and moving into new neighborhoods or being rejected by playmates, belittled by siblings, shamed by adults, and so on. Once we become adults ourselves, we may consider these challenges to be small obstacles, or even insignificant. But a gentle attitude of acknowledgement and support and a few words of encouragement from a parent can be very beneficial at the time and can help the child internalize the strength required to face future transitions.

Eventually, we have to outgrow our need for our mother's protection, develop our identity, and face life. In mythological and psychological terms, this is the heroic journey our personality must make in order to slay the dragon of our dependency needs and become an adult. But what happens when our initial dependency needs were not met sufficiently for us to become internally secure and then be able to separate from them? Or what happens if we have been able to forge only a partial adult identity, which, beneath its surface, hides a wounded one? Then we have to face this paradox of development on a larger scale. We must accept, in a very realistic way, that all new growth within ourselves means giving up the comfort of our present position, even if it is one of suffering. Taking new risks to change ourselves and our lives makes us feel we are also facing danger and suffering, striving for a dreamed-of outcome that we have no guarantee will actually result. It is unfortunate that our culture doesn't know how to support us in these times and doesn't acknowledge that this process is how we grow, because the life-force within us pushes us to grow emotionally, psychologically, and spiritually as long as we are alive.

This paradox is the same one my husband and I experienced. I didn't have a good enough mother and he had a childhood filled with trauma. We both pursued normalcy in late adolescence and early adulthood. While we succeeded in a conventional and material sense, this quest failed us emotionally and psychologically. This failure initiated our need to face our own Medusa, living deeply entrenched in the caverns of our unconscious. Our search began, much as that of Perseus did, in confusion, fear, and a certain sense of hopelessness. But deep in our souls, the Self—the life source within us that wanted to grow—pushed us to seek healing and a transformed life, a life that would take us far beyond normal. Our experience is, very much like Goethe writes, that once we commit to a purpose in life, Providence moves with us. We see that the same took place with Perseus, as Athena and Hermes came to his aid, once he had committed to his journey.

A Deepening Paradox

We face another paradox that crucifies us in this process. If we have had a good enough mother and have internalized a sense of trust in ourselves and life during our early years, this trust should be reflected in our relationship with our unconscious, the source of life within us. As a natural consequence of this trust, we should be confident in our search for self-knowledge—in its wisdom and in its support of our lives and growth. But when we have experienced our mother as the Death Mother in our lives, when we have been mistreated and betrayed by her, then we internalize a basic sense of mistrust in ourselves, in the world around us, and in life. Our early experiences—which should have been ones of bonding, nurturance, and trust—bind us to our fear, fixations, and defensiveness as well as to deep, often hidden, longings for the love and affirmation we never received. People, events, and life find us paralyzed, and significant parts of us are turned to stone. Now we need to take a closer look at how this happens.

We see that the Death Mother gives us a frightening picture of the outside world, but she also gives a terrifying countenance to our own inner world. As long as Medusa is alive in our life, she not only petrifies us but also makes us feel that our unconscious is an enemy, waiting to attack us, diminish us, shame us, and debilitate us. We often wonder if the pain of self-exploration and healing will be more than we can bear, or if the suffering we may encounter is worth it in the long run. In truth, we end up as afraid of ourselves and our inner world as we are of life.

In this sense, the life energy that is supposed to be sustaining our growth has actually become regressive, stagnant, and deadly. This energy reinforces Medusa, like her Gorgon sisters, strengthening the power of her complex within us and heightening our despair, even if we are good at hiding such feelings from ourselves. Our urge to grow may become a negative drive, often expressed as a yearning for peace, a feeling of ongoing fatigue, a longing to surrender, and, in some, an attraction to suicide. There we find the deadly aspect of the Death Mother. Our retreat from this resulting fear of ourselves may have many other forms as well. We may, for example, develop illnesses in which our biological defense systems actually attack our bodies. Or we may rely on antianxiety medications to calm our fears and medications for depression to help relieve the despair we are loath to face. And far too many of us retreat by trying to deny and endure our pain in a world of "normalcy" that may look pretty good but facilitates our avoidance of the inner confrontation and healing we really need. We are in danger of being paralyzed in normalcy. In such a case, the Death Mother has attacked us, and we have given up the fight.

But this is where the myth joins psychology to come to our rescue. Through the mythic pattern, we can see hope and we have a road-map for the journey. The myth shows us clearly the power of life, the sequence of suffering and transformation, and the means by which real courage and real suffering bring us into new life. The myth tears down our illusions that life should bring only happiness and that we should be able to control everything. Further, we discover that if we go through these ordeals consciously, intentionally and pay close atten-tion to the process, we can change the destructive or limiting course we have been on. If, instead, we allow ourselves to take the easier path of living unconsciously, we will face the consequences of the Death Mother's power.

Like Perseus, we may have to wander in confusion before we start our journey to face this complex within us. We need a period to find ourselves, to find our direction, and to find guides to help us. We must confront the Death Mother, but we have to be ready first, the myth says. For Bud and me, our guides have been Jung, Jungian psychology, our Jungian analysis, our dreams, myths, images from the unconscious, and the increasing source of life, courage, and comfort we found within ourselves. We learned to protect ourselves—as Perseus did, using the shield given to him by Athena—to see our Medusa complex by re-flecting, by writing down our experience of her in our journals, and by looking at dreams that may show her presence in our lives. We also hope this book and the help we are offering in it will be a guide for you.

Turned to Stone

Now let us come back to the myth of Medusa and see the effects of her paralyzing gaze. As Perseus approached her cave, he saw men, women, and animals standing like statues in the fields and by the road he was traveling on. They had been turned to stone at the sight of the dread Medusa's face. In a similar manner, over the years, I have worked with woman after woman who was intelligent, capable, even professionally trained, and yet was still paralyzed when it came to pursuing her life with a sense of authenticity and security, grounded in her own ability. I am even more saddened to see how our ability to love and be loved and to be whole people in relationships has been frozen by the Death Mother's influence in our families and in our society. Not only have I seen this in the people I work with, but I have experienced it myself. I have questioned my own ability to believe in myself, in my potentials, and in my own success, not for years, but for decades. And I have wondered if I would ever really know what love is and if I would ever really experience it.

The effect of this paralysis is, therefore, very potent and very frightening. It has the ability to numb our capabilities to be productive, energetic, creative, and independent without our becoming fully aware of it. I have worked with women who were unable to finish college or graduate school because they were "paralyzed," and with women who had chosen to get married, not out of love, but because they were "paralyzed" and couldn't figure out what else to do. Moreover, the Death Mother limits our capacities to trust love and friendships as well as life. And all too often we, both men and women, unconsciously try to heal ourselves by seeking a good enough mother in our spouses, lovers, or partners.

I have also worked with a number of women who became professionals, supported by the courage of the times, but could not bring their creativity and energy fully into their lives. In many cases, these women were haunted by the images emanating from the Death Mother. Such images spoke of shame, incompetence, and not deserving success. These feelings are especially debilitating when they are unconsciously projected on bosses, colleagues, competitors, and other people with authority.

In a similar vein, I have been very moved when working with women who truly wanted to bring love into their homes but were paralyzed even there by the pressure of negativity that they have inherited, which boils deep within their souls. In many cases, visions of their unhappy mothers and clichés of women's roles in the 1950s and before cloud their vision of their possibilities today. With our history in this regard, a history I have shared that I was deeply affected by, this clichéd, shallow image of the feminine caused too many of us to see being quiet, receptive, and, at times, passive as capitulation to a destructive patriarchal system. This was an accurate assessment of the surface of our society. But looking on a more profound level, we can see that the elemental aspects of the feminine are the holding vessel for love, creativity, and the nurturing of a true love life. I think that much of the rage in our souls boils at the way the patriarchal social character fails to value women's efforts—and those of men as well—to bring love into our homes. The Death Mother has also robbed us of models of whole, mature adults being in love, struggling, and growing together.

From another perspective, I have had women colleagues who would say, "I want to stay very quiet and see only a few people." This attitude may be very legitimate, and it often seems to be honoring the feminine. But there is also a real danger in it, because it can just as likely be a fear-based paralysis that can keep even a Jungian analyst from living her true destiny.

Bondage and Fixation

We might wonder how the power of this paralysis can keep a woman or a man connected to the source of such self-destructive negativity. What binds her or him to the Medusa/Death Mother within and to the person that carries this image in the world? Perhaps we never got the love and affirmation we needed in early life. These unfilled needs, which began before we were old enough to figure what was happening, became internalized in our growing personality as an unconscious feeling of emptiness, a general lack of something essential in our world. As a result, we seem to become caught in an overall feeling of *scarcity* that says, "What you've got is not much, but why risk the little you have?"

The Death Mother creates a theme of scarcity in life: feelings we won't be understood, won't get enough love and care, will never have enough money to feel secure. We feel in constant danger of ending up poor and alone.

Perhaps we fear confronting the relationship we have with the image of our mother within ourselves, because unconsciously we feel the weight of the powerful Mother archetype, which has tremendous influence in how we experience ourselves and life. We are often left with a great secret hope of getting the tenderness, warmth, nourishment, understanding, compassion, and love that will never come from this person. In these circumstances, we long for our mothers to value us. All too often we cannot accept that we want our mothers to personify and fulfill the characteristics of the Good Mother archetype, and thereby to heal us. In the face of such hope and longing, we find it hard to realize that she may not be capable of doing this or that she may have no desire to do it.

Many of the women and some of the men I've worked with have continuous trouble seeing their mothers for who they really are. They want to care for their mothers and nurse them as they age. They want to ignore how unpleasant their mothers are and hope that kindness will change the behavior. It is so easy to hope for peace and reconciliation through trying to understand them and their history and to "forgive" them, rather than hold them responsible for their behavior. We have to admit to ourselves that this instinctual hope is stronger than reason and reality. It is like a hope that never seems to die. It is romantic, consoling, and it is praised by our culture. This hope becomes a misunderstood waiting that appears patient, understanding, and wise. In reality, however, it is toxic, like pure poison, the poison of Medusa.

In many situations I have worked with, people think they can free themselves from the Death Mother by trying to forgive their real mothers. Personally, I tried forgetting first, and then forgetting on top of forgiving. There are two problems with this approach. First, it ignores the reality that we have internalized the Death Mother as a complex within ourselves and that she is also part of our broader societal picture. Projecting her outside of ourselves and onto our real mother is too simple a solution. Yes, we must deal with our real mother, but we must also make the inner journey to confront our Death Mother complex and the Death Mother complex in our social character. I will share more about how to work through this confrontation in upcoming chapters.

Second, this approach fails to recognize that forgiveness is a profound activity. It took me some time to accept how significant and meaningful the complexity of it is. Forgiveness and reconciliation are deep psychological processes that, even when spiritual, have an archetypal structure. We see this structure reflected in the sacrament of reconciliation in the more formal, liturgically oriented Christian churches and in the process of making amends in Alcoholic Anonymous. The key to this archetypal process is for the offending person to take full responsibility for the wrongdoing, to express sorrow and regret, and to promise his or her best efforts to not repeat such actions. The archetypal process shows that unless there is an admission of responsibility, forgiveness is an illusion that we create in order to avoid confronting the reality of our experiences and the depths of our feelings, which may seem overwhelming and frightening to us.

Most of us struggle for a long time either trying to get our mothers to live up to the positive side of the mother archetype or trying to excuse them for not doing so. I did this for many years before, in my inner work, I learned how to face the reality I had lived through. These struggles enabled me to build up the frustration and strength to confront the truth of my experiences with my mother. After that, I began the journey into learning how to be a good enough mother to myself, learning how to nurture and affirm myself, and learning how to reassure that deep, injured part of myself that she could trust me now and that I would love and protect her.

Many of the women I have worked with have been terrified of facing the anger that, like Medusa's mane of snakes, writhes deep inside of them. We all fear that this rage could easily overwhelm us, paralyze us or possess us, and destroy the relationships that we value most. Still, we must make the inner journey of seeking out the Death Mother complex within us, of slaying and transforming our Medusa, in order to become healed and renewed ourselves. Once we have completed this journey, we will discover where to put our real mothers, their place in the stories of our lives. Whether we accept or hate them probably won't make much difference, because we will no longer be projecting onto them and tying up our energy in them. Even if we end up hating them or someone else, once we have fully worked through our rage, grief, and woundedness, we will be able to hate without a need for retribution, and this issue will no longer demand a charge of energy from us.

The image of Perseus carefully entering the cave, slowly moving into the dark and using the reflections in the shield given to him by Athena, gives us a good model for approaching this scary rage. We should respect these strong, inner feelings and not try to confront them aggressively and too directly, but steadily, carefully, and through reflection. As we do this work, we are dealing with forces that make up the foundation of who we are. Even the hero Perseus needed to build up strength and exercise caution in this pursuit. A good Jungian analyst, or depth psychotherapist, can be a useful guide and a helpful shield in these circumstances.

And yet the writhing snakes of rage are only the first of the strong emotions we may have to face. Marion Woodman shares with us the gnawing sense of fear we may feel when we realize that we are not pleasing people or that they disapprove of us. She says it is as though our very cells were imprinted with a fear of shame, rejection, belittlement, and abandonment. Sensing these things is like seeing Medusa: We close down, becoming numb and overwhelmed with feelings. These, too, are like Medusa's snakes and must be approached with great care.

It encourages me and sustains me on my journey to remember that although snakes inspire fear in us, they also can inspire awe. They symbolize primal instincts and feelings that are demanding to be transformed. When they are transformed, they become a source of life, like the power of the kundalini serpent, the healing they represent on the caduceus, and transformation they symbolized as they shed their skin. So, I remember that while this journey must be careful, it will be filled with awe at times, not just fear, rage, and grief. And the outcome will be one of love, in its largest sense.

106

Chapter 8

MEN TURNED TO STONE—
CONFRONTING SHAME

Life shrinks or expands in proportion to one's courage.

– ANAÏS NIN

Success without fulfillment seems to be a common denominator in our society. We saw in June Singer's article "The Sadness of the Successful Woman," written over twenty years ago, that many successful women, through their depression and lack of fulfillment, were mourning for their lost femininity. My husband and I still see many women, and men as well, who fall into this category. These women are examples of how, if we as women live too much the spirit of our patriarchal world, we can become successful while unconsciously ignoring, denigrating, or failing to realize our feminine selves. In many cases, we have identified with our animus, the term Jung gives to the masculine component in our personality.

As I mentioned earlier, thinking about human biology can help us grasp Jung's concept of our personalities' feminine and masculine sides. A man has the X, or female, chromosome and female hormones, such as estrogen. Similarly, he has a group of psychological characteristics that form a minority feminine element in his personality. We picture this feminine side of a man's personality as his anima. And a woman's body produces a small quantity of androgens, or male hor-

107

mones. A woman's personality, likewise, has a masculine side that we picture as her animus. These ideas help us differentiate and understand ourselves better. They are important because the Death Mother in our culture creates a basic wound in the foundation of a woman's personality and a wound in a man's anima. If we experience the Death Mother through our personal mothers, these wounds are compounded and a basic wound in the development of a man's personality results as well.

When a woman's animus develops in a healthy way over her lifetime, it helps her have the inner strength to find healing, to support her own voice, to move into the world with purpose and direction, and to develop her intellectual and spiritual capacities. When a man's anima develops in a healthy way, it helps him become open to his feelings; to be in tune with his inner values; to feel "animated" and energized in his life; and, through reflecting on his experiences, to know his inner depths and develop his spiritual capacities. Of course, when these parts of ourselves are wounded as we grow up, there are many ways they can turn negative and need to be healed and transformed and to have their energies transformed, as we will see as this book goes on.

We might also imagine Perseus as an image or a symbol of our animus growing in our personality and helping us find strength, healing, and inner transformation. We can also imagine that the professional women in Singer's article who identified with the spirit of their times, the patriarchy, internally identified with their animus. When a woman identifies with her animus, a minority portion of her personality dominates her identity at the expense of her wholeness and potentials for fulfillment. There is no question that this portion of women's personality and engagement in life has needed to be honored and liberated for centuries, and in reality, we are not there yet. In truth, this part of ourselves, the animus, needs to have a prominent seat at the table in our personality, but it doesn't need to be at the *head* of the table.

These reflections remind me once again of Erin, the gifted nurse that we talked about earlier, whose mother was dominant and highly anxious. As Erin struggled through early childhood, she had to make great efforts to get any of her needs recognized and met, and she compensated for the fear of life she had unknowingly inherited from her mother by acting like she wasn't afraid at all. As Erin grew into her school years, she became a perfectionist to hide her vulnerability and a pleaser to protect herself. She learned to identify with her animus, to get affirmation through her accomplishments and by accommodating others. When I met Erin, she suffered from a growing depression, the consequence of her internal anger and the need to face her rejected and uncared for feminine self. She needed to bring healing and nourishment to it and to give it an active place in her life. Her unmothered feminine self was calling for recognition. Her animus, which had carried her into life, needed to relax, to no longer be driven by her anxiety, and to find its true home in the makeup of her personality.

Andrea comes to mind as well. While working hard to build a life and take care of her children, she lived alone inside of herself. Deep within she was struggling like the sole survivor of a shipwrecked childhood, adrift on an ocean empty of love. Andrea's wounds were more painful than Erin's, even though their efforts to grow and survive were similar. Andrea didn't even think about being loved when she was growing up. She was the oldest of three children and was responsible for her siblings and her sick, alcoholic mother, while her father traveled in his work. With the help of her animus, she endured and worked hard. Enduring and working hard became the dominant theme in her life. As a single mom, she had raised two children and worked her way through college. When I began seeing Andrea professionally, we quickly figured out that she had been depressed all her life. Andrea's story is a good example of the practical effects of the Death Mother; it illustrates how the Medusa can secrete herself in our personality.

The unmothered part of herself—which should have become the internalized ability to nurture herself—had been so violated that it instead became a Medusa, a negative complex in the underground hollow of her personality. This part of her, unloved when it should have been nurtured, filled her with depression, despair, and rage in high school. The scars from cuttings on her arms mirrored her inner reality. Because Andrea felt unworthy of being loved, her relationships never had a chance. Yet a spark of life in her supported her love for her children and her desire for a more enriched sense of living. Like Erin, she needed to find the feminine—the most deeply wounded and denied part of herself, her inner Medusa—and, by healing and transforming it, make it the core of who she could become. She also needed to let her old animus, which had supported her endurance, retire. A new animus, her own Perseus, would support her healing and transformation.

Margaret, another woman I previously mentioned, was on a similar but perhaps more arduous journey. We have seen that Erin's mother was anxious, scared, and insecure, and Andrea's mother was sick and an alcoholic. As mothers, they were distant and destructive, but their failures were somewhat passive. Margaret's mother, on the other hand, was a very active personification of the Death Mother. She was socially on the go, upper middle class and appearance conscious. She was also cold and distant, stern and critical. Nothing that Margaret could do was good enough for her. While Margaret was very intelligent and worked hard in school, doing well and at least finding some affirmation there, her mother never acknowledged any of her successes. When Margaret had some desperate outbursts during adolescence and sought affection from boys in the wrong sorts of ways, her mother accused her of being a failure and crazy and sent her to a series of psychiatrists during high school and college.

The Death Mother that Margaret faced and later internalized left her feeling that she didn't have the right to be happy, to have her own ideas, to love someone, or to expect love in return. And yet, even at midlife, she couldn't let go of her mother and she was still torn up by their relationship. She wanted to make it work, even though she knew her mother would never change. She wanted to take care of her mother and help her have a comfortable old age. Yet she also knew her mother had no interest in having Margaret participate in her life. In all of us affected by this complex, the Death Mother leaves a deep well of longing that cannot be filled as long as we project our needs onto a real person who is incapable of filling them.

Margaret's intelligence took her into a fairly successful life as an editor. But, not surprisingly, she had two failed marriages. And even though intelligent and competent, she lived in constant fear, because when she was faced by critical authority figures anywhere in her life, she would break down in tears and lose her composure. At other times, uncontrollable periods of weeping would overcome her and she would freeze. Then she would accuse herself, blame herself for being a failure and crazy. Margaret had learned to fear her emotions, her nightmares, and the terror and depression that gripped her. In other words, her unconscious, her inner world, frightened her just as much as her outer world, perhaps even more.

When I met her, Margaret saw no hope of healing or transformation within herself, and so she was caught in desperate cycles of anger and despair. It took us a long time and a lot of healing to awaken the Perseus within her and thus to start the quest for transformation. Our way of life today—with its emphasis on appearances, identity, happiness, and security coupled with its distrust of emotions and the inner life—has repressed our urge to heal and grow to our full capacities. But this urge is still within us. If it is nurtured, if like a seed it can find its place in the fertile ground of the healing feminine, growth and a new life will bloom. And this growth and healing took place for Margaret.

Paralyzed Fathers

Success without fulfillment, of course, occurs in men as well as women. This situation can also affect several aspects of our lives, which include not only our careers and personal relationships but also our efforts at parenting our children. Just to make this picture a little more complicated, we might also imagine that the care and attention we give our children can also symbolize our capacity to nurture our own potentials. Further, drowning our children in care and attention may serve as a defense against the fear that living and becoming the person we are meant to be arouses in us. And if we are cold and distant with our children, as Margaret's mother was, we probably regard our growth potentials in the same way: with a paralyzing fear of facing ourselves and life.

But we can't say all of this about mothers, daughters, and sons without considering where fathers fit into these different pictures. We need to examine the father's role in our experiences as well as the mother's because these roles are always intertwined and interdependent. For example, the father whose mother had a Death Mother complex must struggle to heal himself. Otherwise, he will fail to be a good enough father to his children. Also, he may be emotionally overdependent on his wife or have a deep anger at women, which although often concealed even from himself is generally sensed by his wife. Or he may be generally distanced and detached.

It is too easy to think that the role of the good enough father is to be personal, caring, and nurturing. Of course, some degree of these things is important. But during a child's early life, the archetypal role of the good enough father can be compared to providing robust walls that surround and protect a city in a loving but strong embrace. Outside the walls is the unfamiliar: wild beasts and other threatening forces. While inside the city walls are the home, the vegetable garden, the market, familiar faces, the protected ground where a family can be raised in safety. In my father's generation, this safety was primarily thought of as physical and economic. But as our society evolves, we must also add the dimension of emotional safety to this list. Physical, economic, and emotional safety are all necessary to foster growth, and in the long run, a lack of the emotional safety that needs to be provided by fathers can be devastating.

Therefore the father's role is to defend and protect the delicate task of the mother, which is to use her love, intelligence, energy, and patience to nurture her child. To explore this idea further, let's consider the analogy that the mythologist Joseph Campbell uses to describe the archetypal nature of fatherhood. The analogy involves the social structure of chimpanzees. Campbell points out that the role of male chimps is to find food and provide a protective covering for the mother chimps. The mother chimps can then turn their full attention to bearing and nurturing their children. This analogy reminds us that fathers collectively have a societal role to play as well: an inherent responsibility to provide physical, economic, and emotional safety for our families. This crucial masculine role, in too many ways, seems lost in our version of the patriarchy.

We have already considered how a mother who is nervous, anxious, depressed, resentful of the birth, or not appreciated herself will lead her child to feel out of adjustment psychologically. Her child will have a personality founded on a deep sense of anxiety and mistrust of the world. The good enough mother is, in comparison, sufficiently gentle, loving, and emotionally secure. She will help her child to develop a sense of trust in life and in his or her place in the world. During this crucial period, the father's fundamental role will be to provide the mother with the grounding love, peace, and security she needs to be a good enough mother. And if she, like Margaret's mother, is not being a good enough mother, he will have the strength and awareness to intercede and confront her, on behalf of the child.

It is interesting to note that the archetypal role of the good enough mother cannot be projected onto a nurturing father. Archetypally, the roles are not interchangeable. However, this does not in any way mean a woman must stay at home and be a 1950s-style housewife. Nor does it mean a man shouldn't be nurturing and able to take on child-care responsibilities. In the mother's case, I am speaking primarily of the love and ambiance her presence engenders, even if she works or pursues a career. In the man's case, I am emphasizing the sense of safety, particularly emotional safety, that he brings to the family situation. What this line of thinking does mean, however, is that our society should respect the roles of parents more, so that they will be more physically, financially, and emotionally secure—as they are, for example, in most European countries. To work toward this goal, we must first confront our culture's Death Mother complex, which emphasizes cold, bottom-line, impersonal power. For example, we must allow parents to take sufficient time off from work for labor, delivery, maternal bonding, and recovering from childbirth. And during this time, parents should be free from the anxiety of not being paid, losing their jobs, and not having good health care. Failing at these tasks indicates the absence of a "good enough" societal fathering and will create more instinctual wounds to mothers and children, thus feeding the Death Mother in our culture.

Men Turned to Stone

At this point we might wonder what it looks like for a man to have a Medusa complex in his personality. In most cases, such a man is paralyzed by his negative anima, the Death Mother in his own feminine side. He is paralyzed by his feelings, particularly by negative feelings, and he fears their overwhelming strength. When a man's anima is frozen, he often reacts with over-sentimentality in some moments in life. He might burst into tears in movies and on sentimental occasions, even during events he isn't personally connected to. In addition, he might have outbursts of temper and seem overly distant or overly touchy to people close to him.

Men with a Death Mother wound have a deep, even hidden fear that they are incompetent. They usually live with a low level of depression that goes unnoticed for years or decades. Men with a Death Mother complex are also afraid of women, especially of confrontations with women. Such a man resents his partner's unhappiness. As a consequence of his fear, the man relies too much on thinking and rationality. We Jungians tend to explain this situation by saying the man's negative mother complex overwhelms his anima, and thus much of his personality.

I remember a man I worked with many years ago. He was a well-known professor in a prominent medical school. He had become very successful because of his highly refined capacity to think, but he was unable to confront his wife and children or to give guidance to them. His relationships with them were becoming increasingly troubled because even though he was very generous with them, they claimed that trying to deal with him was like trying to deal with a ghost. Even at work, he could not confront his colleagues or act on his feelings and values. This unfortunate man was emotionally paralyzed and was continuously violated and diminished by other people, especially some who envied his success and academic achievements.

Another man I remember clearly had become successful because he was very intelligent and creative. But he could never sustain his success because his Death Mother complex made him severely self-critical. His attacks of self-reproach produced severe anxiety, which resulted in his obsessively overthinking everything he did, and left him paralyzed in the way he related to people.

A third example illustrates the diverse effects the Death Mother complex can have on a man and his anima. This man was living in a small set of rooms over the garage behind his house. He was living there because the relationship with his wife and daughter had become impossible. They had become increasingly cruel and abusive toward him. He could not see that he was creating the Medusa situation outside of himself because he refused to confront his life and these issues within himself. The more he was paralyzed and self-diminishing, the angrier and more aggressive his wife and daughter became with him. His inability to ground himself and to face himself in an effort to emotionally engage in his life caused the atmosphere in his home to become cold, charged with resentment, dead, and hopeless.

Each of these men had an unhappy marriage. Because the anima had been turned to stone, each man was unable to give structure, confidence, or emotional security to his family and children. The anima was dominated by the negative mother complex. In each of these cases, the negative mother complex also kept the masculinity in a stunted state, since a well-developed masculinity comprises more than simple rationality. The Death Mother was truly devouring the lives of these three men and severely damaging their families.

At this point, let us return to Timothy, the successful attorney whom I talked about previously, and learn how he was wounded and how his anima became petrified. You may recall that at first, Timothy had thought he was brought up in a normal family. His father had been an attorney and later a judge. And although his mother had been a homemaker, she had been more occupied with social causes and her tennis club. She had never been available for Timothy. While his material needs were met, his emotional needs—his need for love and affirmation—were ignored, and his mother's interests always came first. He remarked that he wondered if she even liked him. After growing up and getting married, Timothy was unable to confront his wife. Similarly, he could not stand up for himself during their divorce, when his wife was demanding a lot of alimony.

In Timothy's situation, we see the effects of the Death Mother on several levels. To begin with, she supports the patriarchal values that approved of his father's focus on professional achievements, which kept him emotionally distant from his family and uninvolved with their day-to-day lives. He failed to model a mature man in a family relationship, and he failed to provide a safe, protective atmosphere for Timothy to grow up in. To create such an environment, Timothy's father would have had to confront his wife about her unwillingness or inability to help bring an atmosphere of love, safety, and affection into this home. Had Timothy's father known more about himself, his feelings, and his own values, he might have been able to talk to his wife about the values they were living as a family. He, as Timothy's father, would have also been setting a good example for Timothy, showing that it is possible to confront a woman and initiate a deeper relationship with her.

Timothy's mother sought identity affirmation through the approval of other people and accomplishments that gained their esteem. Once again, we see the identity-oriented, the external-accomplishment-oriented perspective that has dominated much of our patriarchal society. The reality is that though both of Timothy's parents probably thought they loved him, he was valued only as an object. Timothy was appreciated only for his grades, his achievements, and not causing his parents any trouble. As a result, during his early years Timothy did not internalize a personal sense of value or a view that the world is a safe place. His distant father and his cold mother caused him to grow into life with a basic sense of fear. Timothy also lived with a low level of depression that came from not receiving the early love and care he needed. No matter how much success he achieved or how much money he made, he lacked confidence in himself and his value to other people. He seemed to believe that his primary value to his family was as an earner and that if he just made more money, everyone in his family would be happy.

Now let us consider how the Death Mother, working through his mother, affected Timothy's anima, his own feminine side. A man's experience of his personal mother imprints on this important aspect of his personality. In a similar way, a woman's experience of her father is the foundation for her animus, her masculine side. Timothy's mother was cold and in effect absent. He learned early, he said, to try to ignore his needs for love, support, and affection. In other words, he froze his anima in her tracks as he grew into adolescence. His attractions to girls

116

were late and few. His marriage was based on a neediness that no marriage could fulfill. His alienation from his capacity to feel, to really experience his emotions, left him unable to truly engage in life and love. A man whose anima is frozen cannot even realize what his needs are, much less articulate them or his authentic values. As Timothy began to face this reality and search into himself, like Perseus beginning his journey, he realized that his whole life could become different.

At this point, it may be helpful to talk about shame. Feelings of shame seemed to be at the heart of Anton's problems. Anton, another man that I mentioned in chapter 1, had created a cover story of passivity for himself. But buried beneath this exterior and his need to be a pleaser was a deep sense of neglect and insecurity. These feelings had grown as his anima had remained locked deep in his unconscious and denied her rightful function—to create a spirit of animation and aliveness—in his personality.

As we might expect, his shame was a symptom of a need for inner transformation, a life that was truly his own and a personality that was larger, more congruent, and intact. You may remember that Anton was a middle-aged biology teacher. His third marriage had just ended and he had two children from his first marriage. He missed his children and felt distant from them, and he despaired of ever being able to have a loving relationship with a woman. Anton thought of himself as a nice person. He didn't often get mad and he tried to keep his interactions pleasant. We also saw earlier that his mother had been the more influential parent in his life. She lived in a world of turbulent emotion and had been determined for him to become a minister or a doctor. Anton had no interest in either of these professions, but the driven needs that fueled his mother's ambitions for him affected him from early in his life. He felt an ongoing sense of failure because he had not become what she wanted, what she needed, and had caused her a certain amount of sorrow. Of course his father, who had worked in an automobile assembly plant, had slowly withdrawn from his family into a mild form of alcoholism and spending time with his friends.

In response to his mother's emotionality and driven unhappiness and his father's failure to give him a safe place to express himself, Anton

117

learned to deny his feelings, so much so that he had trouble recognizing he had feelings at all. I remember he once said, "I *think* I may have a feeling…" which I thought was a funny but accurate way of describing his situation. He just assumed that he wasn't upset, angry, or hurt until his depression—his wounded anima, like a furious Medusa in a deep, inner cavern—became so severe that he had to seek help. His Death Mother complex, his negative mother complex that was buried deep in his unconscious, was sapping his energy and his ability to experience his emotions and to engage in his life. Early in his analysis, Anton had no idea what was happening to him. But he did have some interior intuition that his depression could not be solved by medication alone. He realized he wasn't living the life he was meant to, and even though he was confused and scared, he began his journey, like Perseus, into a new life.

Women and Men Turned to Stone

From the lives of the people I have been sharing with you, we see how powerfully our experiences of the Death Mother become woven into our lives. Her influence on our culture is profound. And for those of us who have also endured the Death Mother complex in our upbringing, these experiences become a theme in our lives, part of the foundation of our personalities. Over time, they take a normative form and become the story of the negative mother or Death Mother complex that dominates our lives.

The Death Mother in our culture wields a cold, devouring power that, as Marion Woodman says, penetrates us body and soul. The Death Mother poisons our wells of hope, drains the energy from our souls and spirits, and leaves us immobilized in a bleak countryside of depression, busyness, denial, and, often, illness. As we have seen in our examples, this force is at its most destructive when it comes from someone we were born expecting to love and trust, our mothers. The wounds turn us to stone in many ways; the spurned, rejected potential person that we are meant to be is locked away in the inner recesses of our psyche, raging and waiting to be faced and transformed.

We lose the sense that life has a profound meaning because in both women and men, the foundation of who we are meant to become has been fractured or is inadequate. We haven't learned to really trust love, particularly of ourselves and life. We cannot deal honestly, thoughtfully, and lovingly with ourselves or others no matter how much we long to. The Death Mother costs women their chance to grow in a balanced way, to confront their inner and outer reality, and to have compassion for themselves that is born of the knowledge gained from their own torments and struggles. In a strange sort of paradox, this wound is easier to see in women than in men, because women in recent times have been in the more vulnerable position in society and because more of the cultural focus has been on them.

But we are a long way from truly facing this wound in our society and in ourselves, much less taking the needed steps to heal it. The Death Mother wounds the basic identity of men as well, leaving them confused, insecure, unable to really feel at home in themselves and life. The compensatory posturing of a patriarchal society—chest-pounding materialism and driven achievements—ultimately fail to help men find a satisfying life. My husband, Bud, has written an important book for men, and women too, *Resurrecting the Unicorn: Masculinity in the 21st Century*. The book describes how we can heal our world's increasingly diminished masculine spirit, which has been the victim of the Death Mother's forceful influence.

When the Death Mother's influence is experienced from our personal mother, it can keep the animus, the masculine energy in a woman's personality, from ever getting off the ground. Or if the animus does function, it arises in a wounded, unbalanced way that can make a woman successful in appearance while leaving her feeling unfulfilled and even unloved and unlovable as a person. A similar thing can happen to men. When their identity and their anima are wounded, they too can grow in an unbalanced way that leaves them appearing successful while feeling unfulfilled, searching for love, and only dimly realizing their life is going wrong.

Jung writes, "Where love reigns, there is no will to power; and where the will to power is paramount, love is lacking." Where the Death

Mother lives, "love is lacking," and in fact, an understanding of love is rarely even present. Yet "love is lacking" describes the denied conditions of our collective world. The presence of this force in our lives robs us of the great feminine values we need to live, both within and outside of ourselves. The Death Mother crushes the ability to love, nurture, and affirm ourselves and new life; the ability to foster transformation of ourselves, life, and culture by being emotionally engaged in life and devoted to it; and the ability to make Eros, the feminine principle of love and relatedness, a central value we live by. These are the potentials for healing and a renewed future that make undertaking our journey, as Perseus did, worthwhile.

Chapter 9

MIRRORING THE DEATH MOTHER
UP CLOSE

*The unconscious wants truth. It ceases to speak to those
who want something else more than truth.*

— ADRIENNE RICH

So far we have taken a brief look at the effects of the Death Mother, the need we have for a good enough mother, and the myth of Medusa, which reflects the pattern of the Death Mother's development. We have also seen how these effects branched into folklore, into psychological projections, and into several people's lives. Now I would like to bring some of this material closer to home by examining the shadow side of mothering, which exists even in good enough mothering and in the roles of good enough parents.

People who believe they had a good or even perfect mother may think they are off the hook. But that is not the case. Our shadow sides in Jungian psychology are the parts and potentials in our personalities that we like to keep out of our personal awareness. Generally, these things are laden with emotions and become powers or forces we neglect and try to keep unconscious. Some of our shadow characteristics operate to balance our one-sided approach to how we define ourselves and to our behavior. Others reflect wounds and repressed potentials that can become increasingly emotional and destructive, as Medusa did.

We have seen that good enough mothers don't need to be perfect. They simply need to be sufficiently gentle, loving, and emotionally secure in order to help their babies develop a basic sense of trust in life, in themselves, and in their place in the world. With a little bit of thought or imagination, we can see that being a good enough mother takes a lot of energy. And being human, we all, even good enough mothers, experience moments of despair, frustration, anger, fatigue, and even bitterness. Being a good enough mother includes living in a very intentional way and denying many of our own emotional and physical needs and desires. As a result, both our egos and our shadows are left with a certain amount of frustration and even resentment at times. Ideally, we as mothers will be aware of the things we are denying ourselves, thinking of them as things we are consciously and knowingly sacrificing to the new life we are nurturing, a life we feel is more important than these particular personal desires. When I say "important," I mean the importance of the mother's taking care of her child and creating her home as a container of her love. Of course, such sacrifices are never perfect, and our efforts at them always build up a certain amount of shadow energy, fatigue, and resentment. For instance, we often see the good enough mother's shadow reflected in our fairy tales (the wicked stepmother) and in our nursery rhymes. Let me mention one example that most people know, "Rock-a-Bye, Baby," a nursery song that is sung sweetly but says

Rock-a-bye, baby, on the treetop,
When the wind blows, the cradle will rock,
When the bough breaks, the cradle will fall,
And down will come baby, cradle and all.

If we look at this little song literally, it becomes rather horrifying. But if we realize that it is really compensatory to the fatigue and stress of being a mother, we can also imagine how it is emotionally supporting mothers while soothing infants. Returning to the image of a mother like Margaret's, however, we see that her destructive energies are much more than a little compensatory energy from her shadow. They are part of the Death Mother complex that both possesses her and is very active in her personality. Consequently, the attributes of the Good Mother that are denied and repressed deeply into her shadow are in her unconscious and unavailable to her children.

The fact that the good enough mother is repressed into Margaret's mother's unconscious does not mean that Margaret has any hope of changing, healing, or redeeming the destructive aspects of her actual mother's cold and damaging behavior. Her mother's attitudes toward being a mother are dominated by her Death Mother complex. Even if Margaret learned to understand how her mother had been wounded and had developed her dreadful approach to parenting, Margaret would still have to deal with her mother's behavior and its effects on her throughout her life. We are often tempted to sentimentally defend, forgive, understand, or relate to destructive parents—or to forget the reality of their cold or cruel treatment—rather than to face the effects they or their memory still have on us. In truth, when people are as possessed by a complex and are as destructive in their behavior as Margaret's mother is, they are also totally convinced that they are right. Such parents believe that there is nothing wrong with them and that they are responding to their child's problems—problems the parents have in fact created or projected onto their child with no self-awareness and with a feeling of justification and superiority.

Knowing that even a good enough mother has a shadow side helps us as mothers—both to our children and to our own potentials—realize that not being perfect is OK. We must also keep in mind that the healing journey is for us to take. The more we heal ourselves, the better we are able to mother our potentials and our children, to renew the life of feminine values and characteristics within ourselves and ultimately within the culture.

Positive Mother Complexes

We have talked so much about negative mother complexes and their extreme version in the Death Mother complex that it now makes sense to ask, what about the other side of the coin, positive mother complexes?

On the surface of things, having a positive complex, especially a positive mother complex, might seem like a good thing. It may certainly be less painful to be in the grip of a positive mother complex than a Death Mother complex, but the result is that we are still not our own person. Any complex that we have not worked through, healed, and integrated works in one of two ways. It can be like a sore, infected wound lying beneath the surface of our consciousness. When we have a certain kind of event arise or a painful or significant encounter with someone, the complex that is sensitive in this area will take over our personality, and we will be living in the expectations, behaviors, emotions, and imagery of the complex. We will suffer a loss of freedom and will be compelled to live the program of the complex, instead of being able to make our own choices. One example of this type of possession that we have already discussed is paralysis caused by the Death Mother.

The second way an untransformed complex, whether positive or negative, can affect us is by becoming a core or central complex in our personality. The examples of the Death Mother we have presented are this kind of complex. These complexes hold our personalities captive. They control our view of life, ourselves, others, and our expectations. We may live as Danaë did in the beginning of the Medusa myth, locked away in a room by her father, whom we may think of as a tyrannical negative complex. Or we may think of Polydectes—the king who gave her and her son, Perseus, a place to live safely—as a positive complex that likewise began to become despotic. Whether we are held captive by a positive or a negative complex, we are being restrained from realizing our sense of aliveness and from generating our own thoughts, feelings, and choices; our capacity to love and relate to others is limited, as is our ability to accept love. These complexes are the king in the landscape of our personality, which means we are dominated by our wounds and may unconsciously see them as ordering our lives and protecting us, even as they rule our responses to life and our perspectives.

A positive mother complex is often caused by a woman who has overly identified herself with the archetypal Good Mother. This type of mother will initially fulfill the good enough mother qualities. But as her children begin to grow up, she will, generally out of her own neediness, continue to mother them as though they were young. She is what we commonly refer to as a smother mother. In many of these situations, the children tend to remain forever immature and to some extent forever touchy and in rebellion. More often than not, they also vacillate for many years between the need for independence and the unresolved dependency needs fostered by their mother.

We encounter an interesting paradox when we see the results the Death Mother can have on her children. Although she may be cold, distant, and even mean and devouring, she may also inspire the formation of a positive mother complex. Let's look again at Erin, the pediatric nurse who was a pleaser and a perfectionist, as an example. Her mother had been the dominant parent in the home and had been highly anxious, cold, and distant. Her mother was also a very busy and successful real estate agent. Erin learned early in her life that the best way to get along with her mother was to please her and do everything right so as to cause her as little trouble as possible. She also idealized her mother's financial success. Erin hoped someday to open her mother to the possibilities of warmth and caring. In her romantic life, she searched out men that she hoped to transform in the same way. She also seemed to often end up with female bosses that she experienced as aloof, aggressive, and degrading, as the complex imposed its pattern on her life. Our need to make other people happy, comfortable, and harmonious, our need to please, is a major characteristic of a positive mother complex. Erin gave the appearance of having a positive complex. Yet as we looked into her life more deeply, we saw that her pleasing and perfection were symptoms of a much more profound set of issues.

Timothy, the lawyer, initially appeared to have a positive mother complex also. Like Erin, he had to please his parents to get any attention at all. Timothy grew up despising any kind of confrontation and became a high achiever to gain his mother's approval. Constantly trying to make everyone happy, he ended up frustrated and depressed. He had no real idea of what he wanted from his life or how he truly felt about almost anything. Being a pleaser, a high achiever, and a perfectionist at work, Timothy had the symptoms of a positive mother complex. However, the deeper issues of the Death Mother complex were robbing him of the love and satisfaction he needed from his work and relationships.

A few years ago Rob came into our offices to see my husband, Bud. Rob was a tall, slender man in his late fifties who carried himself easily. He had been a physician for several decades. When he started to tell Bud his story, he explained that he was beginning to feel trapped in a depression that although wasn't too serious, wouldn't seem to go away. As he continued his story, he caught Bud's attention when he said he visited his mother in a nursing home every day and referred to her as a woman who had been wonderful and devoted to her children. Rob had a wife who ran an antique shop with his support and four children who were grown. Even in his first hour of analysis, Rob brought a warm atmosphere into the room. Rob seemed like an amiable, intelligent, good man, yet he was locked in the cave of his psyche by the tyranny of his complex. Even though this was a positive mother complex, it was destructive to Rob's life, like the Death Mother, and he was imprisoned by a paralyzing depression.

Marty was a woman who, early in life, seemed to have faith in life and the world. She believed she would be recognized at some point as special or outstanding in either her work or relationships. As her life went on, she continued to live with, and later take care of, her mother. Like Rob, she felt it would be a sin to "abandon" her mother. As she entered middle age, she began to become depressed and bitter. Her attitude seemed to ask, is this all the thanks I get? In fact, Marty was never really able to differentiate her identity from her mother's, and her mother didn't want her to. As a result, Marty had an immature sense of self and a repressed longing for her own life, and this longing boiled over into a severe depression and bitterness, as she approached fifty. Other women with such a positive mother complex may simply switch it over to a husband or partner whom they will remain dependent upon.

Our complexes are surprisingly strong forces in our personalities. And although I believe it is helpful to see examples of them in people's lives, it is impossible to show how many forms they may come in and how many feelings they may evoke. For the sake of clarity, I've made these examples somewhat simplistic and extreme. But they reflect the more complicated reality Bud and I see in our practice. It is also a surprise to realize that a positive mother complex that looks so good on the surface can be just as tyrannical and deadly as a negative one. In reality, an unresolved positive mother complex is part of the Death Mother's kingdom. Just like a negative complex, it robs us of our vitality and personhood and is responsible for some of our depressions, anxieties, and narcissistic tendencies, such as delusions of grandeur and oversensitivity to others' opinions.

Reclaiming Our Understanding

At this point, we should remember that the myth of Medusa and this book describe a journey of healing, growth, and transformation. We begin the quest by realizing that an important part of ourselves, the part I call the feminine, is in exile in our psyches and is struggling for existence in our personalities. We must go back into the darkness and experiences of our wounds and of our society's wounds in order to clean out some of the infection in our psyches, in our personalities, and in our hearts.

This journey so far has been intense. But re-creating ourselves requires us to face the reality of our stories, our lives, our experiences and to experience our history fully, possibly for the first time. By doing all of this, we are simultaneously re-creating ourselves and building the foundation for our steps toward transformation in the next three chapters. Before proceeding, we will review seven of the Death Mother's significant effects on us, crystallizing them and amplifying them. We are going back into the darkness of the Death Mother's cave to search for the golden sword of Chrysaor, the vitality of the winged horse Pegasus, and the healing elixir from Medusa's blood that Perseus liberated.

Seven Effects of the Death Mother

The first significant effect is that we project our Death Mother complex as a shadow or dark anima figure of our own. As I mentioned earlier, we can do this in several ways. We can project these negative, critical aspects of ourselves, which disempower and diminish us, onto lovers, spouses, relatives, bosses, churches and other institutions, or even governments. Very often, these projections are so powerful because they also give us a feeling of being good and superior. They enable us to feel justified in our sense of righteousness and feeling victimized and resentful. Now it is also important to realize that whenever there is a projection, there is also a hook for that projection. In other words, some small characteristic in the person or institution corresponds to, or hooks, the characteristic being projected.

For example, we live in a patriarchal society. Our partners can have bad moods, and so can our bosses. And our institutions can be impersonal and diminishing. So I think you can see that there are many small, and not so small, hooks out there. But when we project the Death Mother—the cold, mean, devouring, poisonous, diminishing, and annihilating characteristics—onto these hooks, we do two things. First, we give the people or institutions an overwhelming amount of power over our lives. Second, we simultaneously disempower ourselves and lose our ability to deal with these people and situations effectively.

At that moment, as we empower them, they will feel our distress, animosity, or aggression. When they feel attacked, they will either want to fight back or withdraw, which results in both sides feeling hurt, diminished, or even enraged. Soon we will reach a point where the behavior of both parties is motivated by anger and a desire for power, certainly not by love and respect.

Earlier in the book, I shared with you that for many years, I thought I had a wonderful mother and a happy childhood. Until I deconstructed that illusion, I could not accept the fact that I was a Cinderella in my own family, and I had been unable to see this reality and stand up for myself appropriately. This theme occurred not only in my family life, it also became dominant in any other relationships and situations that had close personal dynamics. This was my core complex. It dominated me and my perspectives, and I projected its dynamics— my family dynamics—whenever similar hooks appeared.

As I mention my own experience of being a Cinderella, it brings to mind the second significant effect, which is the one of paralysis. I certainly experienced paralysis while I was in that complex, and many women, like me, are or have been paralyzed. I also want to mention again that a man can be paralyzed by his negative anima, the Death Mother in his feminine side. This complex causes him to be paralyzed in and by his emotions in general. His negative, self-critical, ambivalent, or depressed feelings are particularly debilitating, and he fears their disruptive and overwhelming strength. Throughout his life, he lives with at least a low level of depression. He is afraid of women. He is especially terrified of confronting women and, and as a consequence of his fear, he relies on his thinking function and rationality or avoids emotional exchanges. If pushed too far, he may have outbursts of rage or simply walk away.

This Medusa complex also stunts the man's masculinity. A well-developed capacity for masculinity is much more than simply being rational. It includes the ability to relate through feelings and stay grounded in emotional situations and confrontations. The Death Mother devours the hearts of men, drains the vitality from their lives, and severely damages their families.

Now let me return to the issue of how paralysis affects the lives of women. As I mentioned earlier, a woman can be intelligent, capable, and even professionally trained and yet become petrified when it comes to pursuing her life with a sense of authenticity and security grounded in her own ability. The effect of this paralysis is very important because it numbs our capacities to be productive, energetic, creative, independent, and confrontational in a positive way. As I mentioned, we see examples of this kind of paralysis in women who are unable to finish college or graduate school because they become paralyzed and in women who choose to get married not out of love but because they can't figure out what else to do or because they want to feel grown-up, secure, and not alone.

When we feel paralyzed in these kinds of situations, we often unconsciously try to heal ourselves by seeking a good enough mother—someone who is always understanding and supportive—in our spouses, lovers, or partners. Another example that I frequently run into is the woman who became a professional, supported by the courage of the times, but cannot act when it is time to bring creativity and energy fully into her life. Other women struggling with this complex may be paralyzed by the pressure or the negativity that they have inherited from their families and that boils deep within their souls.

The third significant effect I want to share is that of giving up. Frequently, we give up without even realizing it. We began to give up as children, when we learned to go with the flow of our families and the values of our society and its institutions. Frequently when we succumb in this way, we think doing so will allow us to live in a secure place. In reality, this place is a state of mind below our potentials. And living in this way—which doesn't make room for our imagination, our individuality, and our needs to be known and loved for who we are—will drain our vitality and creativity. For example, our cultural perspective, or so-called conventional wisdom, is generally a one-sided point of view based on scarcity and fear of disapproval, rejection, shame, or being thought selfish, weird, crazy, or just not normal.

When we give up and choose a life of comfort over hunger for challenges and adventure (whether of mind, body, or spirit), we forget audacity and courage and settle for timidity and a false sense of security. We also forget that to love and to be loved call for courage, taking risks, and living creatively. Some people spend their entire lives in this defensive psychological condition and become fossilized in this state of sleepwalking through life.

The fourth significant effect that I want to emphasize our internalization of the Death Mother's poison. We take in this poison while we are growing up and don't have the mental or emotional maturity and strength to resist it and, in many cases, to even know what is happening to us. This poison symbolizes our sense of being unacceptable to our parents, of being resented by them. As a consequence of our experiences in this regard, our nervous systems becomes hypervigilant and our personalities become withdrawn and defensive. Then as soon as we encounter any hint of confrontation or rejection, we close down—we may even feel a sense of inner collapse—and become frozen. Without having any choice, we find ourselves repeating the emotional survival mechanisms we used while we were growing up. As these old patterns compulsively kick in, we may try to disappear or stay absolutely still, withdrawn or detached, in order not to attract attention. These patterns can also develop into defense mechanisms, such as compulsive weeping, overeating, frequent vomiting, padding ourselves with extra weight, or having migraines or some other physical symptom. Our symptoms are a symbolic effort to keep the poison out and to avoid dealing with our core issue.

The fifth major effect is scapegoating. As you may recall, in the myth Medusa was unjustly punished for being raped in Athena's temple; Poseidon, the attacker, was not punished. It is important for us to ask ourselves, do we feel, as women or men, unjustly punished or diminished?

Women, over the centuries, have been unfairly victimized, misused, belittled, and considered to be inferior human beings. This blaming and belittling of women, and also of the feminine principle, still goes on in this century and in some countries is a common way of dealing with women. Unfortunately, this is our modern form of the plague.

In a similar way, men scapegoat their own feeling selves and, all too often, make fun of other men who express feelings, thus scapegoating the feminine inside and outside of themselves. In fact, men are scapegoated by their own moods as well. Their negative and often critical anima, their inner Medusa, makes them feel that they are inadequate and that their ideas and accomplishments are insignificant. Men have to discover their own inner path for Perseus, in order to take control of their moods.

The sixth important effect is very common and very key in our orientation to life. The Death Mother leaves us with a deep inner feeling of *scarcity* that permeates our feelings about ourselves and life. In this situation, both men and women feel that the world is not a trustworthy place, that deep inside we don't have enough resources to prosper, that life will not support us, and that other people are out to take advantage of us. This perspective leaves us feeling insecure and always trying to be in control of or to micromanage our lives. Such a defensive posture toward life inhibits our ability to love and makes mature love untrustworthy. This foundation of insecurity makes us, like a child, want to be loved unconditionally. Mature love may be accepting, but it is not unconditional.

The seventh significant effect, one that is very consequential, is the issue of rage. As women, we have, I believe, all been taught to repress our rage. But when rage is repressed, it builds up into a larger and larger pool in our unconscious. When I first began to get in touch with my rage, I was afraid that I would be overwhelmed by it if I confronted it. I also feared that I might destroy myself, hurt people I cared for, and demolish things I had worked hard to build or achieve. The same is true for men when they get in touch with this rage in their anima—the anima they have projected onto women personally and collectively for centuries. Far too many men that I have seen in analysis were afraid of women's disapproval, of women's cutting remarks, and of women's anger. In reality, this fear means these men are unconsciously afraid of the unhappiness, discontent, and rage in their own anima.

A Moment for Reflection

I am aware that some aspects of all of these seven effects probably have deep resonances in most of us, so I invite you to spend some time reflecting on them, writing about them in your journal. I believe it is important for us to carefully chew over and digest material like this as we pursue our journey in re-creating ourselves. As I journaled, I would ask myself some questions, like these, about each effect:

1. Which of these effects has been most present in my life?
2. Which one affected my mother or father the most?
3. What are some areas where I have experienced them—in school, at work, in relationships, and so on?
4. What was the primary emotion I felt when reading about each effect?

As we reflect on these questions and on what we have learned about the Death Mother complex and its effects, we are facing the truth of our lives and realizing that we have been living in exile outside of our real selves. The kind of awareness we are developing is hard, but our awareness is the only thing that can form the core of our personal development and begin to free us to live our full vitality and creativity.

Conclusion and More Reflections

When we have been wounded by the Death Mother, we also have to ask ourselves these questions:

1. How can I trust love?
2. Do I know how to love myself?
3. Am I able to receive love?

The truth is that we can't genuinely love someone we do not know, and this includes ourselves. When we don't know ourselves, we relate to other people primarily through projections. This means that our relationships are controlled by our wounds and complexes, and even our notions of love often reflect needy psychological pursuits, idealistic fantasies, or sentimental hopes. Without a great deal of self-knowledge, we will relate to ourselves in this way. We will project onto ourselves, in terms of our self-image, self-esteem, and what we think we are.

The first act of self-love is to seek to know ourselves, which requires undertaking the serious work of confronting our wounds, to start to heal them, and of confronting our shadow. The shadow, the unlikable and repressed parts of ourselves that we don't want to admit to, frequently includes some of our best potentials, which may threaten our status quo. For this reason, these qualities have been denied and treated in shabby ways. This process of seeking self-knowledge lets us learn what our major wounds are, what our major complexes are, and how they are driving our lives. We must develop self-awareness to see how these very complexes are often pushing us to seek solutions to their symptoms in anxiety-driven, shallow, and meaningless ways that will never bring true healing and transformation. Instead, they will tend to increase our dissatisfactions with ourselves and life.

When we are suffering from the Death Mother wound, we frequently project our negativity onto ourselves, and we can get stuck in these projections—these and the projections that "I am unlovable. I am undesirable. I am not worthy of being loved. If I risk love, I will be rejected, even devastated. I am in danger of always being alone, and that will be terrible."

Think about what I am saying here:
1. How can I trust love?
2. Do I know how to love myself?
3. What do I project onto myself?
4. How much do I fear rejection?
5. How much do I feel alone?

Once again, I invite you to reflect on my ideas and these questions, see what they bring up in you, journal your responses, and let your responses provide the context for you as we move into the next chapter and transforming ourselves and our lives.

PART
FOUR

The Freedom to Come Home

And there we have it; the fundamental contradiction and challenge of creativity. If we practice it, we enter the inner world, we find ourselves outside the perimeter of conventional society—outsiders feeling all the loneliness of that disconnection. And yet we are simultaneously as far as we can get from loneliness because we are finally with ourselves.

— Deena Metzger

Chapter 10

A MAP FOR THE JOURNEY

*Truly it is in the darkness that one finds the light, so when
we are in sorrow, then this light is nearest of all to us.*

– MEISTER ECKHART

In 1984 I left my family, my country, and my professional life to go to
Zurich to study at the C. G. Jung Institute. Like Bud and most of my
friends there, I went with very little money, but I had faith that I was
on the path and that "helping hands" would rise up to support me. I
was called to this path by both my inner suffering and my inner convic-
tion that I could find a bigger and richer life than I could imagine. And
if the truth be told, I was as scared as I was excited. Every life, if it is
going to be fulfilled, is a journey. It is a journey from one state of being
to another. It is a journey through the death of an old way of life into a
new one. It is a journey that parallels a woman's giving birth—we must
go with the pain, for to resist it increases the tearing and hinders the
birth. This kind of journey, which is no stranger to suffering, becomes
one of transformation, healing, growth, and the realization of a life that
is beyond what we could have imagined or planned.

Part of this journey, as we saw in the reflections I invited you to
make in the last chapter, is to return to our past many times in order
to pick up the different threads we left behind because of our pain,
carelessness, or lack of awareness. And, let's face it, all of us would like
to simply put painful or unpleasant experiences behind us and move

on with our lives. But doing that would make us shallow and discon-
nect us from our deeper selves and the human family. So we have to go
back and weep the tears we didn't weep, feel the grief we denied when
we suffered losses, and greet our younger selves with the compassion
and love they really need. We may also have to revisit some of our past
accomplishments, letting ourselves take the pride and delight in them
that we were too modest to experience at the time.

Reflecting on our lives, picking up the threads, helps us see the pur-
posefulness in every event in our lives, even if we don't particularly like
our fate. Reflections like the ones I invited you to make will enrich our
lives—though, like the birthing mother, we may have to experience
some pain first.

The myth of Medusa and the story of Perseus bring some of the
threads of life together, too. Medusa is thrown into her journey by fate.
Perseus enters his naively, but he becomes an instrument of the destiny
that transforms Medusa's blood into the giant Chrysaor with the golden
sword, Pegasus the winged horse, and the elixir to be used by Asclepius,
the god of healing. We have thoughtfully examined the details in this
story, for they each have their meaning for us. This myth is crucially important to our work because it offers us a sense of inner clarity about the
situation we face in our personal and collective experience of the Death
Mother. In the myth, we see where the Death Mother comes from and
an example that shows us how to deal with her. The myth can help us
find inner clarity, which becomes like a companion that gives us purpose
and direction, points out new paths, and opens new doors. Using this
approach has transformed my life and my husband's, and the men and
women I have worked with felt that it immediately helped them get new
traction in their lives, providing new hope, a clear understanding of their
situation, and a new direction to pursue.

As I think about the Death Mother as a power and image within
the dynamics of our society and myself, I find it helpful to view her
as a psychological complex. And complexes, you will recall, must be
recognized and transformed. And while this journey of transformation requires Jungian psychology and our own experience, it requires
the archetypal feminine as well. We must bring acceptance, endur-

ance, devotion, and emotional engagement into the journey. From the feminine perspective, we are entering into a process of transformation that is healing, renewing, and nurturing. We are not trying to define a problem and come up with solutions, either through techniques, will-power, or medications. Our complexes are part of who we are, and we want Eros, the feminine urge to nurture, to be our guide as we work toward transformation and unity within ourselves. We have seen that reflecting on our lives and considering the myth of Medusa are helpful companions in our work. I am also going to add a five-step process that will serve as a third companion for our journey. This process encompasses Bud's and my psychological perspective as well as our experience working with ourselves and other people.

We are called to meet and face our Death Mother complex by our circumstances, frustrations, and suffering; by our desire for a more ful-filling and complete life; and by our hope to help create a world that values life and love. It is encouraging to know that women and men have traveled this path before us and that we don't have to plunge blindly into the unknown. Although our path must be unique, it can be guided by a chart, such as the myth, but not by a rigidified doctrine or set of techniques.

As we face this journey, we all have some legitimate questions: What will we encounter? How do we strengthen ourselves for the struggle and the pain? What will the pain be like? What are our alternatives? Is there a map for the territory? What is the reward?

In reality, every complex, like this one, releases new energy into our lives, broadens and strengthens our personality, deepens our ability to give and receive love, adds to our wholeness, and affects the world by changing how we relate to everyone around us. Further, the new inner clarity we develop will refine our ability to see reality in a more accurate way.

In terms of a map in addition to the myth, the series of five steps I have created will guide your work on the Death Mother within you, helping you transform her into the healing and vitalizing energies that came from Medusa's blood. These steps combine Eros and transformation and show us that we do not undertake the journey of

Perseus by trying to overcome Medusa with power, strength, or force of will. Rather, we must diligently follow the steps that lead to transformation and use our aggression in the service of life and wholeness, not against the symptoms of a suffering part of ourselves. I will briefly mention all five of these steps, and then I will develop and amplify them one at a time.

The first step is to recognize our denial of this wound and the depth of the wound's place in our soul. Second, we must accept the reality of our lives, giving up denial and illusions, so that we can heal our pain and live in the truth of our own reality and potentials. The third step is to strengthen ourselves before confronting our Medusa and to realize that this is a labor of love. Fourth, following the path of Perseus, we will do our healing and our inner work, going deep inside ourselves as a labor of love. The fifth step is seeing the transformation take place as we die to our old, false life and are born into a new life. If we do not take this crucial fifth step, we might get stuck contemplating how bad our old life was and how unhappy and frustrated we are today.

❋ ❋ ❋

Step 1: Recognizing Denial

The first thing that we do as small children when our mother fails us is to blame ourselves and internalize a feeling that there must be something wrong with us. So, the first step we should take in working on this Medusa/Death Mother complex is to recognize that we deny or attempt to deny the depth of the complex within ourselves. It is ingrained in us to refuse to believe that our mother has badly failed us, unless her actions have been drastically obvious. The most common form of denial that Bud and I hear is people trying to excuse their mother's behavior by saying, "She did the best she could for who she was." We may also have tried to create the illusion, as I did, that our family is not only a good one but is better than most. Or we may say, "Yes, my family was a train wreck, but I have moved on."

The essence of this process is that we must recognize our denials and illusions, and they must be sacrificed on the altar of our truth. We can think of this as a blood sacrifice in the sense that we must also experience the emotions we have denied and defended ourselves against. In this way, our emotions will be tested against our reality and differentiated from complexes and projections, and so this process can strengthen us further for the journey.

Let's look at some examples to make this point more understandable. You may remember that Erin, the nurse who was initially a pleaser and a perfectionist, had a highly successful mother who appeared to be confident and together. Timothy, the lawyer, had a mother who was active socially and was a visible supporter of many good causes. And Margaret, whose mother was the wife of a surgeon and always gave a perfect appearance, was actually very damaged by her mother's cold and destructive behavior. Erin, Timothy, and Margaret all had to overcome the reality that their mothers appeared great to the world but were Death Mothers to their children.

We recognize the Medusa/Death Mother when we realize our mother, whom we desired to love and whose love and approval we longed for, does not accept us or wanted some part of us or all of us dead or in some way different. If we fear confrontation, disapproval, disappointing someone, or freeze when we are not pleasing people, we know the Medusa/Death Mother is present. As children, we were taught or disciplined as soon as possible to smother our anger, initiative, and creativity and to please, flatter, or avoid our mothers.

Of course our early efforts at survival turn into defense mechanisms. We might constantly please other people, stay anxious and on guard all or most of the time, overeat and surround ourselves with weight, or vomit habitually in our efforts to get the toxic effects out of our system. Chronic fatigue, other autoimmune diseases, and a flow of other physical disturbances can be symptoms that we are overburdened and are unconsciously attacking ourselves. When we are in the grip of these kinds of defenses, we may fear and try to destroy anything that promises real transformation, or we may be driven into endless changes that seem creative and even heroic but never get to the heart of our problem or lead to a satisfying life.

Moreover, the Medusa/Death Mother creates within us a deadly fear of being exposed as inadequate. Because this makes any kind of real intimacy problematic, the Medusa/Death Mother has to be dealt with before we can truly experience love and meaning.

One of the saddest experiences we have as analysts is that we have worked with many people who were unable to look at what they were doing to their children. Many of these parents had some psychological knowledge, and deep down they knew they were failing to be good enough parents. But their own wounds were so strong that they were reluctant to bear the suffering of confronting them and going deep enough in them to find real healing. Therefore, they could not truly change and could not examine how their wounds were affecting their children. Such parents exile their failures into the basement of their unconscious, and in real life they continue to personify the Death Mother's destructive energy. This approach gives the Death Mother more power in their lives, wounds their children, and exacerbates the parents' strong feelings of guilt and negativity. Eventually these feelings in the parents may pass a point of no return. If this happens, the parents will respond with anger and denial to anyone who questions them, including their children as they get older.

We also see this kind of pattern among people in various groups who are studying Jung and learning the Jungian vocabulary but never confronting their deep wounds. The heart of Jungian work is to discover, heal, transform, and integrate our core complex. We must confront our shadow and then change our lives accordingly. Too many people have simply learned how to use Jungian studies and events as a more entertaining type of defense mechanism.

Step 2: Accepting the Reality of Our Lives

Once we give up our denial and illusions about how much the Death Mother has wounded us, we have made significant progress toward our second step: the acceptance of our true reality—not an "objective" reality, but the reality that we experienced and that formed us. Inherent in this

142

process is accepting the reality that we have been damaged by some of the primary attitudes and values in our culture, which we call patriarchal.

Accepting the truth of our experience means that we must learn to look at our lives in a more profound way. We have to see beyond the simplistic ideas in our media and advertising, which tell us that life should bring us only happiness. And those of us who want to cling to the idea that suffering is unacceptable or that we should fight to maintain the positive attitude that our culture idolizes will never experience the fullness of life and love that also have their share of trials and pain.

If we feel the need to fight, defeat, or overcome a symptom or some attitude or characteristic, we have made our complex into an enemy. Consequently, we lose the transformational potentials to which the complex can guide us. Of course this perspective is counter-cultural because it takes the feminine approach to the meaning in our difficulties and how to respond to them. This method makes our ideas of control, rationality, and curing symptoms secondary in our approach to our struggles. If Erin (the nurse), Timothy (the lawyer), and Anton (the teacher) had simply tried to treat their depression in a normal way, they would have lost the potential value in their experience. The Death Mother would have continued in various ways to drain their energy, paralyze them emotionally, and rob them of their future. I am not proposing that we throw out traditional treatments. I am suggesting that if we accept our reality, we must include the feminine and that entails a different way, the way of accepting, relating to, and transforming.

Jung emphatically states that nothing can be transformed until it is accepted. That includes our complexes, our reality, and ourselves. What our inner work demands from us is the acceptance of our true reality. This means we must constantly ask ourselves, what is my true reality? This journey seeks to answer this question. As we re-member our childhood, we are trying to piece together the puzzle of our true reality. And we must reconnect with our emotions, then and now, because our emotions link us to the life we lived or are living and tell us how we experienced or are experiencing it.

So, we must find out what our true reality is in order to accept it. Many of us find it very hard to take a truthful look at our parents and how they affected us. We feel that taking a realistic look at our child-hood is taking a critical look at our parents. And that goes against our societal injunction to honor them. But to take a realistic and "critical look" doesn't necessarily mean we are either judging them or ourselves. We are doing a personal psychological/anthropological search. We are looking at ourselves and our lives in our efforts to give up our denials and illusions, for the love of truth—the truth of our own reality, which we need to accept, even if it includes some difficult experiences and strong emotions.

Step 3: Building Our Strength

The third step, building up strength before we approach our Medusa, is not an easy undertaking. It is a labor of love that we can do with a Jungian analyst or depth psychotherapist that works with us, as a guide, in the same way Athena and Hermes assisted Perseus. In other words, we have to build up our strength before facing this complex. We have to develop our Perseus, rather than just confronting the Death Mother directly. Bud's book *Sacred Selfishness: A Guide to Living a Life of Substance* and our book *Like Gold Through Fire: Understanding the Transforming Power of Suffering* are also helpful guides for this part of the journey.

During this step, we need to learn how to honor and do our inner work of keeping up with our dreams, journaling, and active imagination (see a detailed explanation of this in *Sacred Selfishness*) as sacred undertakings, not as another task we try to cram into a day already crammed with tasks. We must also build up the strength to see that having days crammed with tasks is not being fully alive, and our learning to sacrifice may have to begin here.

Loving ourselves in this way fosters our growth in consciousness and transformation and, in doing this, strengthens and enlarges us. This step helps us learn to be a good enough mother to ourselves, and (like the good enough father to ourselves) we must wall off a space where we can nurture ourselves, gestate new life, and give safe birth to new potentials.

Step 4: Following the Path of Perseus

The fourth step is to learn from the myth and follow the modeling of Perseus. At this point, we have become more aware of our reality and our need to accept it. We have also learned that our healing and inner work must be done in an atmosphere of love and in a sacred, protected space. Next we must venture deeper inside, just as Perseus carefully traveled deeper into the cave of Medusa. We will have to work on our dreams, look at the patterns in our lives, and examine our feeling reactions to people and life through journaling and developing more awareness of what is going on in our bodies. As Perseus descended into Medusa's cave, he walked backward holding the sword of discrimination, which could not be broken. He was guided by the reflections in the shield Athena gave to him. We too have to walk backward into our memories, feelings, and old patterns and reflect upon them so we can build up the strength we need.

There are many parallels we can glean from the myth to help mark our own journey. Perseus went to the oracle at Delphi to learn where the Gorgons could be found. He consulted with Hermes and Athena. Then he went to the Graeae, the gray women, and to the captivating nymphs. As we begin our inner journey, we will learn much from listening to our dreams. We should first note what people and scenes in them carry the strongest feelings for us. Then we can consider what elements in the dream stand out as the most impressive. We also want to ask ourselves what the setting of the dream or the landscape suggests to us. We should also be curious about the characters in the dream and how they may reflect unfamiliar aspects of our own being. Finally, we may ask ourselves, what is my role in the story of the dream?

I also use this format to approach my daily journaling. I pay attention to situations and people that have stirred up the strongest feelings during my day. I want to see what elements in my day stand out as the most impressive. As I ponder, I take note of the people I have interacted with during the day and think about how I might learn from my projections on them. Finally, I reflect on how I see my role in the story of my day.

Margaret, whom I mentioned several times as being very intelligent and who had described her mother as having "an iron fist in a velvet glove," is not an isolated case. When we began to talk about her feelings, she became overwhelmed by her emotions whenever her mother, childhood, or current situations that reflected her early experiences came up. To help her stay grounded, we went slowly in our work and kept the image of Perseus, holding the unbreakable sword in his hand, clearly in her mind and reflections. And it was helpful to her to find a picture of Perseus in a book, copy it, and paste it into her journal. This image reminded her that she had some power, could discriminate or cut things apart, and, in this case, could use her intelligence to sort out her feelings. Shortly after that, she had a beautiful dream of a tiger resting quietly in her backyard. At first, the dream scared her. The more we talked about it, however, the more she began to appreciate that this symbol of feminine power resting in her unconscious represented a potential in her. This image renewed her strength for the journey and, as a sign of inner support, inspired her.

Andrea—the hardworking single mom whose mother had been an alcoholic and had a nervous breakdown, leaving Andrea in charge of the family—had come in to see me when she was in her mid-forties and experiencing a haunting dissatisfaction in her life. As we began our work together, she told me for as long as she could remember, she had been tormented by the fairy tale "The Little Match Girl." This story, from the Hans Christian Andersen collection, is poignant beyond words. It is the story of a poor little girl who is selling matches as she scrabbles for a living in the dead of winter. In her efforts to keep warm, she lights the matches she is trying to sell, and as she freezes to death, she has a beautiful vision of being enfolded in the loving arms of her Grandmother. This tragic story enabled me to begin talking about the archetype of the Great Mother, who is within us and can support us. It also led us to look at the pain that Andrea experienced in having to sacrifice her childhood and adolescence to care for her mother and family. Before Andrea was ready to start journaling, we deliberately journeyed back through her past in order to revitalize the young girl in her. She wrote the history of her childhood as a fairy tale describing a young girl

146

who had a hard life, but also a future. As we spent months on this part of the journey, her capacity to know and accept her emotions expanded greatly, and she began to dream and to journal.

When Timothy, the attorney who had learned in childhood to block his feelings and deny his emotional needs, began this work, he found it very difficult. His dreams were distant, abstract, and mechanical. He struggled to come up with feelings in his journaling. He once commented wryly, "I think I had a feeling." But as he struggled, motivated by his unhappiness with his life and his relationships with his children, he began to discover that simply paying attention to these things was beginning to shift who he was and how he felt about life. Paying serious attention is an important part of the healing process. His children began to notice that he was different, too.

One day when Timothy was journaling, he became aware of how much his best friend from childhood was annoying him. As he continued journaling, he realized that his friend had been an emotionally turbulent person all of his life. Timothy was quick to catch on that he had projected his emotional capacities onto his friend. He also realized that just naming a projection and deciding to take it back doesn't really accomplish very much. Our capacity for feeling, for having emotions, for knowing the values of our heart must be born within ourselves through the careful reclaiming of ourselves, through healing the wounds to our feminine selves. Timothy came to understand this work needed to be deliberate. He had to search for his feelings, express them—even though they may come out unpolished at first—and experience whatever tension and emotional turmoil this stirred up in himself and the people around him. The Medusa myth helped Timothy realize these efforts are worth their price, and he is discovering the life-giving power of the healing elixir that came from Medusa's blood.

Step 5: Seeing the Transformation

The fifth step is to pay attention to our lives so that we can see our transformation taking place. In taking this step, we are doing the work of dying to our old, false life and are being born into a new life. If we do not commit ourselves to mindfulness, we may easily start to live as if we were wearing blinders. We can get stuck ruminating about how bad our old life was and how frustrated we are today.

As we do this inner work, an important part of our reflections is to observe how we put the results of this work into practice, how we live differently because of it, and how these changes transform who we are and how we deal with our lives. It is essential to understand the transformation that is taking place within us, seeing that we are dying to the false, seemingly secure image of ourselves and are bringing about changes in how we are living. We have to clearly grasp this new level of consciousness; otherwise we will easily lose it.

Even in the early stages of her journey, Margaret has to value the image of the sword in everyday situations by setting up boundaries on her feelings, both within and without, and on others who may be too intrusive. She also has to visualize her tiger power as supporting her with fierceness, grace, and beauty in her inner quest and in her outer life. Andrea has to continue learning how to love herself, how to wrap herself warmly in her own arms, and how to use the strength that helped her endure her early life to give a loving and protected space to the girl within her, the girl who wants to heal and grow while she is facing life with renewed hope and vitality. And Timothy must take the risks of experiencing his feelings and expressing his values and his needs. He has to see that this struggle to become himself and to be forthright will not only broaden and strengthen him but will involve him in relationships of substance as well.

* * *

After Perseus struck the deadly blow to Medusa, something unexpected happened. From the blood of her neck, Pegasus and Chrysaor came to life. If we are able to search out and kill the Medusa within us, from that dead vitality, a new energy will come to life. The winged horse, Pegasus, pictures the energy that comes from our efforts, and he represents the instinctual vigor that can carry us strongly through life.

He also symbolizes the power we now have to develop our full psychological potentials. Meanwhile, Chrysaor, the giant, is born holding the golden sword that symbolizes both the power and the value of discrimination. This sword exemplifies the capacities to set up boundaries and to empower our personal journey beyond the constraints of society and conventional wisdom.

Our culture has a hidden contempt for the archetypal feminine values exemplified in the second hexagram in the *I Ching*, "The Receptive." This disdain leaves us in grave danger of overidentifying with the products of thinking, rationality, and achievements in the outer world. Our society fails to appreciate the woman who quietly responds to life with intense interest and with love for people, ideas, and things. Yet these characteristics are as deeply and truly creative as are the characteristics of those who seek to lead, to act, and to achieve. We have a bias against feminine values. Not only are we too busy to adequately nurture our children, but we are also unable to truly nourish *our own* creativity, our personhood, our ability to take a stand for life, and our capacities to love and live from the heart. The feminine qualities of receptivity, nurturing in silence, relatedness, patience, and secrecy (whether in a man or in a woman) are absolutely necessary to offset our society's increasing institutionalization and pressures that leave us too busy to live. We cannot be good enough parents to our children, ourselves, or to the matters of our own heart until we confront the Death Mother's power in ourselves and in our culture.

Determination makes the difference. We must be determined to get over our culture's impatient, quick fix, and get-on-with-it attitude that feeds the Death Mother. We must never give up and never let so-called reasons—Death Mother excuses such as time, money, health, an overpacked schedule, too many obligations, fears about hurting others or being selfish—stop us.

We must come through the darkness so we can "come into the light."

We must be determined to live, to say yes to life.

Chapter 11

FINDING OUR VOICE

All I have is a voice
To undo the folded lie
The romantic lie in the brain
In the lie of authority
Whose buildings grope the sky...
We must love one another or die

– W. H. AUDEN

Over the years, I have become convinced that seeking transformation is the Divine Way. Transformation is the theme not only in
myths and fairy tales but also in all the mystery religions. One of the
oldest of these mystery religions was the Eleusinian Mysteries in ancient Greece, which became the grandmother of the Western mystery
religions and Western mysticism. These mysteries were secret, but
they grew out of the myths and tradition of the grain goddess, Demeter; her daughter, Persephone; the descent into darkness; and the returning transformed. The Greeks believed that going through these
mysteries—which consisted, in effect, of enacting and experiencing
the myth—would transform them in this life and the next. Jungian
psychology sees these stories and myths as rooted in our collective
unconscious, where—if we can pay attention to them, experience
them, and make them relevant to our lives—they can also transform
us. I find it reassuring to remember that transformation, as I pointed

151

out in chapter 1, is one of the two fundamental aspects of the Great Mother.

Although our journeys into transformation often seem to begin out of feelings of hopelessness, pain, desperation, or rage, we must remember that as we follow them, we will discover that joy, appreciation, and gratitude are just as deeply enfolded in our lives. Joy, appreciation, and gratitude cannot themselves be the goal of our seeking. When they are, they seem to get in their own way and distract us from the deeper purpose we are pursuing. Yet the path of transformation releases these very things to us as we pursue it, and they will support and enrich our efforts.

One of the deepest longings in my early life and young adulthood was to be heard. I wanted to speak and have people listen, pay attention, honor, and understand. As I have worked with women over the years, I have come to believe that one of our greatest longings is to have our own voice. I was surprised to find that young men longed for the same thing—or rather, longed for their anima, their feelings, and their values to have a voice. The Death Mother and the patriarchy have silenced the voice of the feminine so drastically that in far too many cases, we cannot hear it within ourselves. We need to recover our voice first, so that we can hear it and then speak it. The following Venetian fairy tale comes from a collection of Italian fairy tales put together by Italo Calvino. It became my personal guide as I recovered my voice, and then it became helpful to many of the women and men I have worked with. I believe that you may find it helpful as well.

Silent for Seven Years

There was once a mother and father with two little boys and a girl. The father was often away from home traveling and one day when he was away the two little boys said to their mother, "We are going to meet Papa!" Their mother replied, "Yes, yes, go ahead."

When they reached the woods, the children stopped to play. Shortly afterward, they saw their father approaching and ran up and grabbed him around the legs, saying, "Papa! Papa!"

The father was in a bad humor that day and replied, "Don't bother me! Go away!" But the boys paid no attention and went on pulling on his legs.

Thoroughly irritated, the father yelled, "The Devil take you both!" In that moment the Devil came out and took them away before the father knew what had happened to them.

When the mother saw the father return without the children, she became worried and started crying. Her husband first told her he didn't know where they were, then he admitted cursing them, after which they disappeared from sight.

At that their little sister spoke up. "Even if it means losing my own life, I'm going to look for them." Ignoring her parents' protests, she got together a little food and departed.

Coming to a palace with an iron door, she went in and found herself before a gentleman, whom she asked, "Have you by any chance seen my brothers who were kidnapped by the Devil?"

"I can't say that I have. But go through that door into a room with twenty-four beds and see if the boys are there."

In effect, the maiden found her brothers in bed and was overjoyed. "So you are here, little brothers! That means you're safe after all!"

"Take a closer look," replied the brothers, "and see whether we are safe."

She peered beneath the bedclothes and beheld countless flames. "Oh, my brothers! What can I do to save you?"

"If you do not speak for seven years, you will save us. But in that time you must go through fire and water."

"Don't worry, you can count on me."

She left them and walked back through the other room past the gentleman sitting there. He motioned to her to approach, but she shook her head, made the sign of the cross, and left the palace.

After walking and walking she found herself in a forest. Exhausted she lay down and went to sleep. A king out hunting passed by and saw her sleeping. "What a beautiful girl!" he exclaimed, then woke her up to ask whatever brought her to the forest. With her head she made a sign that she was not there by her will. The king then asked, "Would you like to come with me?" and she nodded yes. Taking her at first for a deaf-mute, the king spoke loudly, but shortly realized she could hear even a whisper.

He got home and took her out of the carriage, telling his mother he had found a speechless maiden asleep in the forest, whom he was going to marry.

"I'll never consent to it!" exclaimed his mother.

"But here, I make the decisions," he snapped, and the wedding took place.

The mother-in-law was wicked-hearted and treated her daughter-in-law shamefully, but the daughter-in-law endured all in silence. Meanwhile she found herself with child. The mother-in-law forged a letter to her son calling him to a certain city where he was supposedly being swindled. The king said goodbye to his expectant wife and went off to attend to the matter. The wife gave birth to a baby boy, but the mother-in-law, in league with the midwife, placed a dog in bed beside the new mother and took the baby stuffed in a box to the palace roof. The poor young woman looked on frantically, but then remembered her condemned brothers and bit her tongue.

The mother-in-law wrote her son immediately that his wife had given birth to a dog. The king replied that he wished to hear no more about his wife. He ordered that she be given a little money for food and turned out of the palace before he got home.

But the old woman told a servant to take the young wife off, kill her, throw her body into the sea, and bring back her clothes.

When they reached the seashore, the servant said, "Please bow your head now, madam, as I'm obliged to kill you." With tears in her eyes, the young woman sank to her knees and joined her hands. Moved to pity, the servant merely cut off her hair and took all her clothes, leaving her his own shirt and trousers to put on.

Alone on the deserted shore, the young woman at last spotted a ship at sea and signaled to it. The ship carried soldiers who asked her who she was, never once suspecting she was a girl. In sign language she explained she was a sailor from a shipwrecked vessel and its sole survivor. The soldiers said, "Even if you can't talk, you can still help us wage war."

There was a battle and the young woman fired her share of cannon shots. Because of her bravery, her comrades in arms made her a corporal right away. Once the war was over she requested a discharge, which was granted.

Back on land, she didn't know which way to turn. At night she spied a tumbledown house and went inside. Hearing footsteps at midnight, she peeped out and saw thirteen murderers go out the back door. She let them get well out of sight, then went to the rear of the house and found a large table laid for a feast. Thirteen places were set, and she went around the table taking just a tiny bit of food at each place, so that the murderers would find nothing missing when they came back. Then she returned to her hiding place, but forgot to remove her spoon from one of the plates before she left. The murderers came home in the middle of the night, and one of them noticed the spoon at once. "Look! Some stranger has been here meddling."

"Well," replied another murderer, "let's go back out while one of us stays behind to keep watch." And so they did.

Thinking they had all left, the girl jumped out and the murderer grabbed her. "I have you now, you rogue! You just wait!"

Thoroughly frightened, she explained by signs that she was a mute and had come in because she was lost. The murderer comforted her and gave her food and drink. The others came home, heard the tale, and said, "Now that you are here you shall remain with us. Otherwise we'd have to kill you."

Nodding her agreement, she stayed on with them.

The murderers never left her by herself. One day the ringleader said to her, "Tomorrow night we're all going to descend on the palace of a certain king and steal all his valuables. You shall come with us."

He told her the name of the king, who happened to be her own husband, whom she wrote and warned of the danger. As a result, when the murderers started through the front door of the palace at midnight, the servants barricaded there in the dark hall slew them one by one. Thus died the ringleader and five others, while all the rest fled in every direction, leaving the young woman, who was also dressed as a murderer, at the mercy of the servants.

What did they do but seize her, bind her hand and foot, and carry her off to prison. From her cell she could see them constructing the gallows in the town square. Only one more day, and her seven years of silence would be up. In sign language she begged them to put off her execution until tomorrow, to which the king consented. The next day they led her to the scaffold. On the first step she asked them in sign if, instead of executing her at three o'clock, they would wait one more hour. The king agreed to this also. Four o'clock struck and she was moving a step higher, when two warriors came forward, bowed to the king, and begged permission to speak.

"Speak," said the king.

"Why is that young man being sent to his death?"

The king explained why.

"That is no man, mind you, but our sister!" And they told the king why she had not uttered a word for the last seven years. Then they said to her, "Speak up, the danger is over, and we are safe."

They removed her shackles and, in the presence of the whole city, she said, "I'm the king's wife, and my wicked mother-in-law killed my baby. Go to the roof, get that box and see whether I gave birth to a dog or to a baby boy." The king sent his servants for the box, and there inside lay a baby's skeleton.

At that, the whole city shouted, "String up the queen and the midwife in place of this courageous soul!" And so died the two old women, while the young wife returned to the palace with her husband, and the two brothers became prime ministers of the king.

* * *

"Silent for Seven Years" as Our Story

The title "Silent for Seven Years" became very interesting to me because it represents the main character's decision not to speak for a specific amount of time. Her decision was voluntary on the one hand, but on the other hand it was necessary to save her two brothers, a particular part of herself that had been damaged by their insufferable father. This story also reminds me of the great poet and writer, Maya Angelou. In her wonderful autobiography, *I Know Why the Caged Bird Sings*, she writes about being raped as a child. After she was raped, she told who had abused her so severely, and he was murdered, it was supposed, by one of her relatives. After that event, she didn't utter a word for five years. In her book, she explains that as a child, she concluded that her voice had killed him and that her voice could kill if she used it. Maya's story is deeply moving and had a strong effect on me. For most of us, however, the situation has been completely different—opposite, I'd say. We learn early to silence our real voice out of the fear that it could get us killed, emotionally annihilated. I understand this feeling well from my childhood, as you will see, and so did the people whose stories I've been sharing with you: Margaret, Erin, Timothy, and Anton. In the fairy tale, the girl's decision is not to speak for a specific period. This suggests that if she can persevere, a change will take place.

The story begins with a distant father who is returning home in a bad mood and has no time for his sons or the love and potential they may symbolize in his life. The situation goes from bad to worse as the father curses them and the devil comes out and takes them. To be in a bed of flames and locked away by the devil certainly makes me think of how the patriarchy, in such a destructive mood because of the emotional effects of the Death Mother, curses our potentially growing and renewing masculine spirit and how this spirit could bring renewed strength and support to men and women. In the face of this harsh situation, the girl makes a conscious decision to go and look for the path to free and redeem these vital potentials and renew her relationship to them. She makes a choice, like we must make a choice, and it is at this point her transforming journey begins.

This voluntary retreat into herself causes me to remember the time when I had finished my psychological training and had started my new professional life. At the same time, I had been in Jungian analysis and in inspiring inner work. But I had also lost my marriage and clearly was out of step with my family and culture. I felt there was still a lot in me that needed to be rescued and released. So, I left what I had built and went to Zurich to dedicate myself to my inner work in a more intense and devoted way.

When I look back, I realize that my move took a lot of courage. But I am also aware that my determination, like that of the girl in the story, was driven by my desperation to have a life that was really my own. This "retreat" into myself had begun in a less visible way many years before, when I realized that my voice was not heard and not respected in my family. The atmosphere in my home was always negative and critical. It was the result of the strong influence of the Death Mother as she was pictured through my mother and a culture that supported few alternatives for me.

In this fairy tale, the Death Mother's presence is realized in the passivity of the children's mother. She is incapable of living the positive mother aspects that would give her the strength to love, affirm, and *protect* her children. Nor was she able to confront her husband and tell him he had better get those boys back. The Death Mother is also present in the foul mood of the father as she, through his anima, has soured his mood, crippled his capacity to love, and caused him to become destructive.

After the courageous decision to search for her brothers, the girl finds them neatly tucked into bed in a room with twenty-four beds. At first, she thought they were safe, but when they told her to look again, she found countless flames torturing them but not consuming them.

At first glance, she seems to be faced with an impossible task. If I tried to translate this scene into the everyday language I grew up with, I imagine it would sound something like this: "There is nothing you can do to resolve this problem, because to even try would be so awful and painful." In my experience, the dominating atmosphere of the Death Mother affects us like quicksand that silently devours anything that moves with life and enthusiasm. It does this in a methodical, strong, unchanging way. But here is the dilemma we often face: Everything looks good on the outside, yet if we look beneath the surface, we are being constantly tortured. And if we take action, we know we must face the fear of an uncertain outcome. The only thing that can transform the deadly pattern shown here is silent but active determination on our part, being capable of facing the fear that we may lose the life we have become accustomed to. Silence is an important element here, because talking about our deep inner journeys and struggles, unless in the container of an analytic or therapy situation, can work against us; be a distraction; invite other people's judgment, projections, and interference; and cause us to doubt ourselves. In reality, losing our life in these circumstances is more likely to mean losing our illusions as we transform this deadly pattern into a new life we couldn't have set as a goal to achieve.

We can see that even as the girl's journey is beginning, a powerful and fundamental change is already taking place. The silence of the mother, which has been destructive and malignant and has permeated the family, is thrown into sharp contrast with the silence of the girl, which results from a conscious choice that is actually creative and, as we shall see, transforming. We can be encouraged here by remembering that the leitmotif in fairy tales is transformation. They follow a pattern that begins in desperation, followed by fear, then courage, then commitment—a journey of transformation. With the transformation comes new life, new freedom, a feeling of unity and joy, as we see at the end of this story.

As our story continues, the girl enters the forest, a perennial symbol of the unconscious in fairy tales, and falls asleep because she is so exhausted. In our personal experience, whenever we enter the unconscious, we encounter the heavy, thick, dark aspects where we are "alone," not in a sentimental way, but in a visceral, potentially formative way. After waking, the girl soon enters one of life's paradoxes. She is now getting married to a king, but at the same time, she is face-to-face with a mother-in-law who displays her powers by being actively destructive and aggressive toward the girl. Many of us will find that when we are ready to take a positive step for ourselves—starting a new career or business, entering a new relationship, going back to school, or something else—the Death Mother is still with us, and our journey is still only beginning.

The story reminds us that the Death Mother is resilient and can bounce back again and again, until she is killed. In this scene, she shows her deadly power by killing the baby, the new potential brought forth by the girl's marriage to the king. The Death Mother attacks to eliminate the future and possibilities of the girl. I have personally experienced these assaults in many ways that ranged from subtle innuendos to aggressive and diminishing insults. What was so painfully difficult for me to understand and accept was that my mother, who appeared to the outside world as gentle and sweet, was so negative toward me for no justifiable reason. For me, this was a stumbling block that kept me stuck, it seemed, for the longest time. A pitiful, conventional voice in me always said, "But she is your mother. You are supposed to honor her. Be nice to her." This confusion was crippling until I realized that unless I faced the reality of my mother and her effects on me, I would not be able to confront my inner evil queen, who was killing my potentials. These are the realities we must come to grips with if we are going to create a better world for our inner and outer children. We need to create a world, within ourselves and without, that nurtures the new beginnings of life and their spirits as they develop. And while we, and our talents, must become shaped and formed to live and flourish in our culture, we cannot allow our spirits and our authenticity to be killed during this process.

At this point in the story, the girl's journey has taken a definite negative turn. She is banished from the palace, rejected, and sentenced to die. The Death Mother seems to be in control, but there is a paradox here. The Death Mother, at her worst in our culture in the form of over-mothering our complexes or in a man's negative anima, can still fall into positive potentialities of the transformative character of the Great Mother archetype. In other words, the Death Mother, if we can choose to face our lives and ourselves, pushes, kicks, and drags us toward the foreign land of our full independence. I remember that when I made this point in one of my seminars, I heard Timothy say, "Oh my God!" and I heard Margaret say, under her breath, "That doesn't mean I have to like her!"

We are all left to wonder if there is an easier or better way than this cruel and brutal manner. It seems that there are no easy paths, no effortless roads to get to a place of authentic and genuine transformation. The process teaches us that if we can have such troubles with our mothers, our families, and ourselves, we need to accept the brutal and cruel realities of life; yet enfolded in this background are our great potentials for creativity, love, and joy. We can arrive at this position through our dedicated inner work. And if we are having trouble believing in ourselves, we must search for a good analyst or therapist, one who is not caught in the patriarchal web of trying to "treat" us or get us back to "normal," but one who understands transformation can lead to a life beyond normal. It can be difficult to find someone with the psychological wisdom necessary to create a relationship that gives you what you need and helps you find the support within yourself for the next steps. But if we can find the right guide—and Jungian analysts can be good at this—he or she can help us into this new and well-deserved stage in our lives.

Another turning point in the story, a change of scene, occurs when the young woman is in a battle and defends herself bravely. Strengthened by her struggles with life, she has become capable of taking the initiative, being active, and, above all, being unafraid of experiencing and using aggression. I have seen many examples of these creative shifts, when we can begin to stand up for ourselves, survive difficult circumstances and start anew, give up our dependency needs and become able to stand alone, free ourselves from our histories and the Death Mother and become mature enough to give and receive love.

I know how difficult it is for us to find our own voice or, in some cases, to even let ourselves realize we lost or never developed our voice. It is painfully hard to find a way of expressing ourselves that is both feminine and strong but not tainted by harsh characteristics of a negative animus, who is often the "son" of the Death Mother. A man can also have difficulty learning how to integrate and express his anima, his feelings, and his values without having them contaminated by his inner critical witch, fostered by the Death Mother. The course of the next step in our inner development depends upon the continuous choices we make in transforming ourselves. The world we live in pushes us in a direction dominated by one-sided patriarchal values. We must dedicate ourselves to cultivating our inner development like a delicate, beautiful flower and protect it from the surrounding pollution.

The inner drama portrayed by this fairy tale culminates with the girl's encounter with thirteen murderers. The number thirteen indicates that the young woman has achieved a certain level of life's work, as symbolized by the number twelve. The additional one that is added denotes in number symbolism that a new challenge is coming up. In other words, even though she has gained new levels of strength, experience, and confidence, she is not done with her transforming challenges yet. The presence of the murderers in the story, as an inner drama, shows she is still dealing with conflicts within herself. "Murderers" are within her still, killing her vitality and self-worth. In the fairy tale, she is trapped in the murderers' den, signifying her new awareness that her unconscious is full of stolen "treasures" that she is finding the possibility of reclaiming. This scene reminds me of how I discovered the hidden treasures within myself through my dreams and reflections.

In our story, the thirteen murderers were planning to rob a palace that was, by coincidence, the palace of her husband. Now that she has gained more awareness and her psyche has more dynamic energy, she can respond appropriately to the messages of her unconscious. So, she writes a letter to her husband, warning him of the coming danger. This letter begins to repair the damaged connection with him in this inner drama, and she will soon enjoy the results of her reconciling move.

At the palace the guards are prepared, because of her warning, and they catch the murderers and the young woman, thinking she is one of them. As they prepare to kill her, the seven years of the curse are coming to their end. She is able to have her execution delayed for one day and then for one more hour. As the hour ends, two warriors come forward and explain to the king that the young man who was thought to be a murderer, and whom he was about to execute, was a woman, their sister, and, indeed, the king's wife.

As the story ends, she is able to speak up and explain the evil of the queen and the midwife, both of whom are executed. The young woman rejoins her husband, the king, and her two brothers become his prime ministers.

This ending is not simply a rosy conclusion in which everybody is happy forever after. It is the well-deserved accomplishment of an inner transformation. The young woman's hard work brought about an integration of her personality and created a new foundation for her future. This is what the work and the journey to find our own voice is truly about.

One of our greatest longings is to have our own voice, one that speaks of our greatest values with strength, clarity, compassion, and understanding. I want a voice like that and more. I want a voice that can also speak with authority, tenderness, love, joy, sorrow, anger, respect, and humor. I want a voice of my own that expresses the fullness of who I am. And I believe, my husband believes, and the people I have worked with believe that gaining this voice is worth every step in the struggle.

Chapter 12

CHANGING OUR FATE

No trumpets sound when the important decisions of our life are made.
Destiny is made known silently.

– AGNES DE MILLE

As I have looked back over the story of my life, I often feel a sense of awe and wonder because, as you saw in the previous chapter, the events in it reminded me of a fairy tale. In these moments I see my difficult beginnings, and I remember that I have previously described myself as a Cinderella—a woman motherless and disenfranchised—and also as a woman without her own voice. As I opened this book, I shared with you that I grew up in a patriarchal world where my sisters and I had to work to help send my brothers to the university. Like many fairy tale characters, I grew up in a bleak emotional environment. When I can stop my rationally trained professional mind and slip back into the pure, open mind of a child, I can see that I was caught in a spell until I began my analysis. Like the princess in the following fairy tale, something was wrong with my fate.

In fairy tales a person who is under a spell or cursed turns into something else, perhaps a frog, a donkey, an ugly duckling, or a girl with no voice or no hands. To be under a spell may also mean to be asleep, unconscious, caught in circumstances, or bound by some power that is seen as outside of ourselves. What follows is another story like mine; a woman has to undertake quite a journey—not just to find her real self, as in "Silent for Seven Years," but also to change her fate. Fairy tales are maps for the journey, which bring clarity to our minds. And if we are open to them, taking them in through our feminine selves, they become a means of transport as well. They help carry us through our transformation.

As we wander on these journeys, we find that just like in the stories, we often begin in shadowy places, dark forests of the heart or lonely castles that reflect some of the gloomiest wounded and denied places within the kingdom of ourselves. Along the way, we will meet monsters, strange animals (even talking ones), and extraordinary people like dwarfs, witches, beggars, old hags, and even the devil. Some of these figures are helpful; others try to hinder us or even destroy us. But if we want to follow the maps laid out by these stories and to be transported by the stories, we must remember to embrace the world of metaphor because, in reality, the story is within us. The dangers are within ourselves, in our situation and in our unconscious. The helpful figures are parts of our unconscious as well. Psychologically, as you have probably imagined by now, to be in a spell, cursed, or enchanted is to be in the grips of a major complex in our personality. The helpful figures and the guiding plot of the story come from what we Jungians call the *Self.* For us, the Self represents both the center of who we are and the totality of who we are. We may also think of the Self as an integration point, the ground of our being, where the mind, body, soul, and spirit come together. Our perceptions, feelings, personal history, cultural history, and collective history join in the Self. And the Self carries the unique pattern for who we are to become psychologically, creatively, and emotionally, just as it contains the patterns of our physical growth through our DNA. These patterns come to us through our DNA in the same way our instinctual urge to grow into them does.

When our patterns of psychological and emotional growth are blocked or derailed in some way, fairy tales and myths help us find the way back to ourselves and the life we have the potential to live. Fairy tales, in particular, have trouble fitting into the overly rational world of the patriarchy because they don't "make sense." Because they can't be understood or grasped by the overly rational mind, they are threatening, so the patriarchal culture banishes them into the world of children, distances them for entertainment, and tries to make money from them. After all, what would happen if the men or the women who had pursued materialism, success, and a powerful identity began to realize they were turning themselves into the lonely Beast in "Beauty and the Beast"? Perhaps it's better to distance the story, make it into a movie, and try to make money on it than to listen to the message in the story.

But fairy tales fit very well into the symbolic world of the archetypal feminine, where there is the soft consciousness of the moonlight and room for mystery. This is realm of sacred groves; the whisperings of the heart; and the pure, open minds of children. Here the dark recesses of life are accepted. Transformation is a central theme in almost all fairy tales, so they lead us on journeys of discovery and awakening, out of complexes and into individuation—Jung's term for our process of healing and growth into wholeness, consciousness, and the unique pattern that marks our authentic life.

When I first went into analysis, I wondered if there was any hope that the frustration and deadness I felt would end. I wondered what kind of future I could have. The choices and visions of the future I had at the time weren't inspiring to me at all. That is when this fairy tale began to appeal to me for the first time. Today it appeals to me still and for two reasons. First, as the title says, it is about changing our fate, and to know we can do this is very reassuring. Many of the women and men who come to see me are discouraged just as I was. Their future looks daunting and hope seems very distant. I often share with them my experience of taking this fairy tale into my heart. The second reason that I selected this story is that psychologically it gives us an archetypal pattern, a symbolic map that can help us change the fate of the feminine as it is pictured within ourselves. The reality of this map and the opportunity it presents are crucial for both women and men.

My husband and I also think that these two stories give us a change of pace in our personal journey and broaden our perspectives as we work to transform ourselves. Facing the Death Mother and recognizing the control she has on our lives and society is an intense and dramatic endeavor. But for the sake of having our own lives and the love that is available to us, we must strive with all of our heart to slay our Medusa. As we work to face and transform our Medusa, these two stories can help us reclaim vital parts of ourselves—our voice and our lives—which the Death Mother has cut us off from. Bud and I believe they can be as supportive for you as they have been for us. We also believe that fairy tales are less dense than myths and can be more fun. This one describes the same path of restoring our life and our future, but from a different perspective than the Medusa myth. So, we invite you to sit comfortably in the moonlight of feminine consciousness and let us share "The Ill-Fated Princess" with you.

The Ill-Fated Princess

Once upon a time there was a Queen who had three daughters she could not settle with husbands. The Queen thought it a sore burden that other girls should marry, while these, who were Princesses, were all but growing old, unwed. One day a beggar woman came to the palace asking for alms. Seeing the Queen so distressed, she asked what the matter was, and she told her about her sorrow.

Then the beggar woman said to her, "Mark well what I tell you. Tonight, when your daughters are asleep, you must watch and see how each of them sleeps, and come tell me."

This the Queen did. That night she watched and saw that her eldest daughter slept with her hands on her head, the second had her hands on her bosom, while the third folded them in her lap. When the beggar woman came the following day, the Queen told her what she had seen.

Then the beggar woman said to her, "Attend to me, my Lady Queen. It's she who had her hands folded in her lap that is the ill-fated one, and it is her evil Fate that hinders the Fates of the others."

When the beggar woman had gone, the Queen sat deep in thought. "Listen to me, Mother," her youngest daughter said to her, "do not be sad. I heard it all and now I know that it is I who hinders my two sisters from being wed. Have all my dowry rendered into gold pieces and sewn into the hem of my dress, and let me go."

166

The Queen said no, and asked her, "Where would you go, my child?" But she paid no heed. She dressed herself in nun's clothing and, after bidding her mother farewell, set forth. As she was leaving by the palace gate, two bridegrooms rode up for her sisters.

So the unhappy girl went on and on, until at evening she came to a certain village. Here she knocked on the door of a cloth dealer's house and asked him to let her spend the night there. He told her to go up to the best chamber, but she refused and said she would stay downstairs.

That night her Fate came and began to rip up the cloths that were stored downstairs, tearing them into shreds and wreaking chaos all around, for all the girl begged her not to. But would the Fate pay any heed to her? She made her cower by saying she would tear her to pieces as well. At daybreak the dealer went down to see how the nun had spent the night. When he saw all the damage—his wares destroyed, and the house turned upside down—he said to the girl: "Alas, lady nun! What harm is this you've done to me? You have ruined me. What's to become of me now?"

"Bide awhile, bide awhile," answered she, and opened the hem of her skirt, and took out some gold pieces, and said, "Are these enough for you?"

"They are, they are."

And so she bade him goodbye, and again went on her way. On and on she went, until it again grew dark and she knocked on a glass merchant's door. The same happened there. She asked to spend the night downstairs, and again her Fate went in the night and left nothing standing. The next day, the glass merchant went to ask how the nun had spent the night, and saw the chaos that had been wrought. He cried out in protest, but when she had filled his hands with gold, he was appeased and let her go. The unfortunate girl again followed her road, until she came to the royal palace of that country. There she asked to see the Queen and besought her to give her work.

The Queen, who was a keen-witted woman, saw that it was a noblewoman hiding behind the nun's veil, and asked her if she knew how to embroider in pearls. She answered that she was very well able to work in pearls, and so the Queen kept her beside her. But when the ill-fated girl sat down to embroider, the pictures came down from the wall, snatched the pearls from her, tormented her and would not let her be for as much as a moment. The Queen saw all this and was sorry for her.

Often, when the servants came to complain that the dishes had been broken in the night and that it was she who had done it, the Queen replied, "Be still, be still, for she is a Princess and a noblewoman, but she is under an evil Fate, poor thing."

So one day the Queen said to her, "Listen to me, my child. You cannot go on living in this fashion, with your Fate pursuing you, unless you find a way to change your Fate."

"But what must I do?" the girl asked her. "What must I do to change my Fate?"

"Listen well to me. You see that high mountain that seems so far away? On it, all the Fates in the world live together. There they have their palaces, and that is the road you must take. Go up to the very top of the mountain, seek out your Fate, give her the piece of bread that I shall give you, and say to her, 'Fate who decreed my fate, change my fate.' Do not leave, whatever she may do to you, until you have seen her take the bread in her hands."

And that is what the Princess did. She took the bread and went up the pathway until she came to the top of the mountain. She knocked at the garden gate, and a very handsome young woman dressed in fine clothes opened the gate and came out.

"But you are not mine," she said, and went inside again.

After a while, another came out, just as beautiful and fine.

"I don't know you, my good girl," she said, and went away.

Another came, and yet another, and many came out, but none knew her to be her own, until one, disheveled and ragged, torn and filthy, came to the door.

"What are you looking for here, you foolish girl?" she said to the Princess. "Split you, hang you, begone! I'll have your heart out!"

The ill-fated girl handed her the bread, and said, "Fate, who decreed my fate, change my fate."

"Begone! Go and tell your mother you must be born again, put to the breast, and lulled to sleep. Then come here, and I'll change your fate."

The other Fates said to her, "Change her fate, for you have given her an evil one. Is she, a Princess, to be tormented in this fashion? Give her another fate, give her another."

"I will not, so let her be gone!"

At that moment, she took the bread and hurled it at the girl's head, and it rolled right down. The girl picked it up, and took it to her again, and said, "Take it, good Fate, and change my fate."

But she spurned her, and threw stones at her.

At last, with the pleading of one Fate and the other, the girl's persistence in giving her the bread, the evil Fate was obliged to say, "Give it to me," and snatched it.

The girl stood trembling before her, afraid she was about to throw it at her again, but the Fate held on to it, and said, "Attend to what I say! Take this ball of thread," (and she threw her a ball of silk thread) "and take good heed! You must neither sell it nor give it away, but when it is sought of you, you must demand its weight in gold. Go now about your business."

The girl took the ball of thread, and went back to the Queen. Now she was no more troubled.

In the neighboring land, the King was ready to wed, and the bride's dress still lacked a quantity of silk that must match. The people at the palace had been seeking far and wide for something to match. They had heard that in the neighboring kingdom there was a young woman who had a ball of silk thread. So they went and asked her to bring the thread with her to the bride's palace, so they might see if it matched the dress. When they got there, they put the ball of thread against the dress, and saw that it was one and the same. Then they asked how much she would take for it, and she replied that she would sell it only by weight. They brought up the scales and placed a quantity of gold pieces on the other side, but the scales never moved. They went on putting in pieces of gold, but in vain.

Then the Prince himself got on the scale, and then the silk was balanced, so the Prince said, "Since your silk weighs as much as I, then, for us to have the silk, you must have me."

And so it came about. The Prince married the Princess, and there was great joy; they lived well, and may we live even better.

* * *

And so our story has a happy ending. Fate has been changed. Balance, harmony, and potentials for the future have been regained—not easily, not naively but through facing the journey and its challenges. When I finish reading a story, I like to take my time and savor it, review in my mind and see what feelings and images come up freely for me. Then I carefully write them in my journal because I want to keep them with me. Reflecting on the following questions can help guide us into the story on a personal level.

1. Was anything in the story puzzling to you? Did any part of it cause you to feel uncomfortable?
2. Where did you feel energized or engaged?
3. Which character touched you the most?
4. How did you feel at the end of the story?

❊ ❊ ❊

To me, the very nature of this story seems to follow a theme that reflects my feelings about the feminine today. The queen and the princesses are of royal blood, and they and their future are vital to the kingdom. The same is true of the aspects of the feminine, the aspects vital within ourselves. Yet in the kingdom of our personality, they are also abandoned by the king—the strong, energetic masculine—the father, so to speak, of the realm; the future of the kingdom is at stake. We must avoid the mistake of becoming literal here. This is not about gender roles. Rather, this issue concerns the heart and soul of who we are, and if we heal and restore ourselves, working out gender roles will become much easier.

The queen is worried about her daughters' marriages. But the future she seeks for them will continue to be one-sided, unbalanced, and impotent instead of generative, life-giving, and life-supporting. This is a fitting characterization of the destructive grip the Death Mother has on our culture and on our lives. And it reminds me that all of the great feminine values that we have talked about in this book are lying abandoned. Yet in the tale, they are not withering and dying; they are still alive within us, waiting for a future, waiting for a suitor who is yet to appear. This is true of the feminine both in women and in men. The story also indicates that this quest is a feminine quest. Remember that Perseus had to pursue Me-

dusa in a careful, reflective, feminine way and not in the clichéd, powerfully heroic, patriarchal approach to challenges. Masculine and feminine
are both needed, but we must look inward to the feminine because our
patriarchal outer world has become too far removed from the heart of
lives being lived and cannot be helpful.

As the queen waits in distress in her castle, a surprise comes in
the form of one of those wonderfully helpful fairy tale figures: a beggar woman. These helpful figures personify the central force for life in
our personality, the Self. They will help us get organized and find new
directions. Perhaps this beggar woman is also wisdom in disguise, or
perhaps she is a representative of the Great Mother archetype. But as
a beggar—a wretched, impoverished woman—she represents part of
the feminine within us whose wisdom and insight we have neglected.
However, if we pay attention to life and answer the knocks on our inner doors, she will show up to help us. She told the queen something
peculiar to look for, and then she said the youngest daughter's fate was
standing in everyone's way. The youngest child always carries the most
potential for transformation in fairy tales. Transformation not faced—
kept asleep or unconscious, as the daughters were—always invites a
bleak future. The mythologist Joseph Campbell tells us the hero's or
heroine's call, a summons by life, is always a journey toward transformation, and to refuse it invites a cruel fate.

The queen ponders what the beggar woman has said, but she is
reluctant to let her daughter go. She fears for the princess's future. Here
we see that she is a kind mother but, at the same time, a bad mother.
She, in fact, "kindly" gives her daughter away to her fate. The queen
projects the family's bad luck onto her and takes no responsibility for
their misfortune. She hasn't confronted the king or asked the beggar
woman what she could do to correct the situation. The beggar woman
was shrewd enough to see for herself where the real potential lay. It
seems that we are all reluctant to encounter our shadows; they, like the
beggar woman, can force us to face ourselves. Quite often, we have
trouble admitting to ourselves that these embarrassing, annoying parts
of ourselves may contain the seeds of our best potentials and the new
directions we want to take.

The daughter, however, takes a different point of view. She over-hears the beggar woman and decides on the spot that she is leaving. She takes her golden dowry, the symbol of both her social status and her inheritance, the foundation of her future life. Then she dresses herself as a nun and leaves. Therefore, she is taking responsibility for her destiny. Even though she has no idea where she is going, she is full of purpose. This is a feeling we all may share when we really begin our inner quest, but like the princess, we must stay full of purpose. I believe by dressing as a nun, she is focusing on the inner life, in effect, devoting herself to the journey. This approach parallels the way we must enter our devotion to healing ourselves, discovering ourselves, and changing our fate. And in fact, the minute she leaves the castle and starts her journey, two suitors call on her sisters. Their arrival shows that although there are still obstacles ahead, our commitment itself can begin to improve our situation.

As the unlucky princess makes her first stop for the night, she stays with a trader and insists on staying in his basement. So, she remains committed to staying in relationship with her unconscious, especially at night, by remaining below the ground level and at the foundational level. But her bad fortune pursues her still, and rips up the fabric stored there. This event teaches us that starting on the path to our interior depths, where we will become ourselves and find new wholeness, doesn't mean our trials are over. It is also important to note that she doesn't hesitate to spend part of her dowry that is supposed to guarantee her future security. In a similar way, when I left everything and went to live in Zurich, I spent all that I had to pay my way; it was a combination of courage and desperation that served me well. The realization of our authentic lives requires us to invest our time, and sometimes our money. To devote sufficient resources to our journey, we often have to risk the security that conventional wisdom offers.

Conventional, patriarchal wisdom tells us we should know where we are going, why we are going, how much it will cost, and how we will benefit. Feminine wisdom operates differently, however. It says that if we imagine we know where we are going, what we want to achieve, and how to do it, we will fail at our essential task in life. That task is to learn to be open to our Self, the pattern within us—opening to the wholeness the Self wants us to live into and allowing the unity within ourselves to grow and direct us into a life beyond what we could imagine, beyond the normal in our society. Preconceived ideas, goals, and plans are often useful, but they can also limit the power of the feminine in our lives and alienate us from our creative center and the mysteries within ourselves and life.

The next visit the princess makes is to the shop of a glassware maker. Again, she stays in the cellar, and once again, her cruel fate, Moira (a name that means "fate"), comes and wrecks the place. The frustration of the princess must be growing. The glassware may symbolize everything that human hands have crafted with great care will be smashed to bits. In this instance, it may signify broken promises and shattered expectations or the fragility of broken relationships whose pieces need to be swept up. The broken glass also reminds me of the dream I had while writing my lecture on Medusa, in which I had to eat shards of glass. In this story, it seems that our princess cannot hold on to what life offers her. Her bitter fate, like the Death Mother, pursues her relentlessly, and she has to spend her golden coins to offset the losses.

The princess sets an example for us by paying with her own money as she goes and focusing on the present and her journey. She didn't let worrying about the cost or the future hinder her. There is a great lesson here: Even though she didn't personally cause the upheaval and destruction, she didn't hesitate to pay the price for it.

In spite of these encounters with her bitter fate, she doesn't waiver in her purpose. She arrives at a castle and a good queen appears. Now she finds a good mothering influence and reaches a turning point in the story, which shows what happens when we begin to nurture and honor ourselves. The queen immediately sees the princess is of royal blood and sets her to work embroidering with pearls. Embroidery suggests to me the integration of life's delicate fragility with some of its highest feminine values. The pearl is an enduring work of beauty and value that is formed from the grit of suffering. Like silver and the moon, it symbolizes the feminine principle of life. And the pearl emerges from an oyster shell, like Aphrodite, the goddess of love.

173

While this is a turning point, the bitter fate of the princess still pursues her, creating destruction around her at night. The good queen, however, recognizes what the problem is. She tells the princess that she must get a new fate by confronting her old one. The queen has realized that in some unconscious way, the princess is living against herself, in the same way we live against ourselves when we do not seek out and live the potentials within ourselves. The good queen here parallels a good analyst or therapist, who is capable of giving the kind of caring but honest feedback that brings clarity and focus. Like the princess, we too must confront the complexes that control us and determine our fate, as the Death Mother does.

To get a new fate, the princess has to climb to the top of a nearby mountain. The story is implying that we too have to ascend a mountain to confront our fate. We must climb beyond the level of everyday life, even beyond the good life in the castle. We must come to the place where fate and the fates live. We must rise to the point where we are no longer naïve, where we can see both how loving and how cruel life can be. We know now that fairy tales are true and that they are a communication from our Self, from the archetypal world, from the ground of our being. We know this because we are learning how to listen to their symbolic language by opening our hearts.

At this point, the queen tells the princess to give bread to her fate and to be sure she keeps it in her hands. Bread is made by human hands—ground, shaped, kneaded, and baked. It was a great source of life in the ancient world, made from the bounty of the Great Mother, Demeter, or Mother Earth. Bread is a powerful symbol of life, of nurturance, and of the body. Of course, the princess finds her fate angry, combative, dirty, and unkempt. This is an important point: Clearly her fate, like the beggar woman, has not been valued, paid attention to, and given a place in the life of the princess and her family.

If we make a parallel with our inner journey, the gift of the bread could mean that we have to respect our inner life and the images that come from within. We must nourish them by giving them our time and energy: writing down our dreams, dialoguing, painting the images that come to us—even if, or especially if, they are ugly or hostile.

How many of us prefer to sleepwalk through our lives of busyness, obligations, and even fun, hobbies, and entertainment? I'm amused when people ask me, "What do you do for fun?" If we are living a real life, that question is irrelevant. Fun will have its natural place. To change our fate, we must learn to recognize it, to honor it, and to give it bread, nourishment, and body. When I found my voice, confronted the Death Mother within me, and began to awaken to my depths and life—because I wanted to awaken more than anything else—I began to realize that I had a fate, a purpose in my life. My awakening began my struggle with my fate, just as the princess had to struggle with hers. But to awaken to our fate and struggle with it is to honor and value it. We must persist in this struggle until we gain a new fate, a new destiny, and a new meaning in our lives. The Death Mother impoverishes our fate, denies our destiny, and undercuts the meaning available to us as we live.

Finally, the princess's struggle pays off. Her fate relents and gives her a gift, saying, "Go now about your business." Now with a good fate behind her, she continues her journey with the gift of a ball of silken thread from her fate. Elegant, gossamer threads of silk are woven symbolically by the small events in our lives. They are strong and beautiful, the result of self-knowledge clearly earned by accepting the full summons of life, to be committed to our journey of individuation. We feel these silken threads in the smoothness of mature love and in the soft welcoming texture of life beckoning before us.

Through the weight of the silken ball, the princess found a prince; that is to say, she found unity within herself. We might imagine that as the princess and the prince come together, so do the feminine qualities of nurturing, loving, desiring, appreciating mysteries, and wisdom join with the masculine qualities of strength, action, the pursuit of knowledge, and meaning. If we can value our existence enough to follow Perseus and transform the Death Mother, we can change the pattern of our lives. If we can value our opportunities enough to listen and learn from the feminine sources deep within us, we can find the silken threads that bring balance into our lives and create a pattern that reflects our love of life.

The Prayer of Sir Francis Drake

As I was working on my lecture on the Death Mother, I came across this prayer by Sir Francis Drake. I was impressed with how five centuries ago, it reflected the spirit of a man who served a queen and seemed grounded in his masculinity while also being very in touch with his anima, the feminine within himself. I shared the poem with my audiences during my lectures, and it impressed them as it did me. I hope that you enjoy it and find it inspiring, because I believe it also reflects the spirit of the princess who was able to change her fate.

The Prayer of Sir Francis Drake

Disturb us, Lord, when we are well pleased with ourselves,
When our dreams have come true
Because we have dreamed too little,
When we arrived safely
Because we sailed too close to the shore.

Disturb us, Lord, when
With the abundance of things we possess
We have lost our thirst
For the waters of life;
Having fallen in love with life
We have ceased to dream of eternity
And in our efforts to build a new Earth,
We have allowed our vision
Of the new Heaven to dim.

Disturb us, Lord, to dare more boldly,
To venture on wider seas
Where storms will show your mastery;
Where losing sight of land,
We shall find the stars.
We ask You to push back
The horizons of our hopes;

And to push into the future
In strength, courage, hope, and love.

Conclusion

I began this book by noting that something is lacking in the lives of
women and men, and that is a living relationship with the archetypal,
eternal feminine potentials within ourselves and in our culture. Whether
you are a man or a woman, the need to know the characteristics of our
feminine nature—to be able to live them and have them be alive in our
world—is very great. We are called to make this journey so that we might
live in quieter, less aggressive modes, connecting with our more organic
rhythms in a loving ambience. The feminine, which tends to be quieter
and even hidden in today's harsh atmosphere of living, has been suffo-
cated by patriarchal forces. By using the term *patriarchal,* I don't mean
men or even the masculine archetype. Our patriarchy is a one-sided par-
ody of mature masculinity. Bud has written a beautiful book, *Resurrecting
the Unicorn: Masculinity in the 21st Century,* that is opening the road toward masculine wholeness for men. But as the feminine has become en-
tombed, banished like Medusa in a cave, her attributes have turned cold,
negative, enraged—as Medusa did—and produced the Death Mother
complex in ourselves and our society.

We have explored this complex, how it affects us, our culture, our
parenting, and, most of all, our lives as individuals. From this understanding, we have looked to the myth of Medusa and two fairy tales
to search for a way to heal and transform our Death Mother wound/
complex and release our vitality and potentials. We have seen that if we
fear confrontation, disapproval, or disappointing people or if we freeze
when we are not pleasing people or when we are confronted, we know
that the Death Mother is present in our personality. We also know that
she was in the room when we were taught to smother our anger, initiative, and creativity and to please, flatter, or avoid our mother.

Of course, our early efforts at survival and adaptation turn into au-
tomatic defense mechanisms. These are various, often centered on our

Death Mother complex, and can be present in many different ways. For example, they surface as trying to please, being anxious and on guard, or eating too much. We can also show our Death Mother's symptoms by being overweight, vomiting, or having chronic fatigue, autoimmune diseases, or other physical disturbances. In reality, we live all the time with a certain level of fear, depression, and feeling of scarcity—the deep underlying belief we can never have enough to feel fully safe or really have our needs recognized and met. When gripped by these defenses, we tend, like the Death Mother, to fear and try to destroy anything that demands or promises real transformation. Or in a different way, we try to lose ourselves in busyness and obligations. Too often, we are also driven into the pursuit of endless changes—whether physical, spiritual, or psychological—that on the surface seem worthwhile, even creative and heroic. Yet we never get to the heart of our problem, take the demanding path of Perseus, and find a truly satisfying life.

We also saw the fundamental importance of accepting our true reality. Jung said clearly that nothing can be transformed if it is not accepted. We have to continuously ask ourselves, what is our true reality? To find this out, we must return to the beginning of our life's story and re-member the emotional events in our lives and the people in them, because our complexes originate in the feelings of our early relationships. A great help is to journal and question the emotional circumstances in our daily lives. This process of re-membering is not one of judging either ourselves or our parents. It is looking at ourselves and giving up denial and illusion for the love of truth, the truth of our own reality, and the acceptance of our potentials.

Midlife often becomes a turning point: We either accept the truth of our reality or seek safety in remaining asleep, unconscious in our roles in life. One alternative that we have is to choose the path of Medusa's transforming, life-giving blood. Asclepius, the god of healing, used the blood flowing from the right side of her neck to give people new life. In other words, by reflecting on our lives, working on our dreams, being open to our feelings and our unconscious, we can begin transforming the Medusa within us. The other alternative is to choose the vial of blood that came from the left side of her neck, the blood of poison Asclepius used to put people to death. This is to say, by refusing our calls to transformation, we choose this vial and become dead to our potentials; and this choice can, in many cases, lead to hopelessness, bitterness, and loneliness.

The vial of deadly blood sours the feminine soul in a woman and releases the power of the rigid, negative animus, the inner patriarchal tyrant in her life. In a man this same vial releases the souring power of the negative anima, the critical, moody witch that erodes and weakens his masculine spirit. Both men and women, in this case, can be living on top of a repressed or not-so-repressed volcano of rage and bitterness that frequently erupts in depression, fear, and illness.

If we are going to face our personal and cultural reality, we cannot continue to busily dance through our lives in denial, as though nothing has happened. We must realize that something singularly awful has happened. We have lost touch with the meaning and values of the eternal feminine—how love can live in our lives, support them, value them, and transform them. As a result of this loss, the inner journey of individuation, of healing and growth into wholeness, seems too radical and challenging today for far too many people. But, in fact, it is a traditional way of transforming and transporting life forward, and it is born from our Western healing and spiritual traditions and the feminine mysteries of transformation that go back to ancient Greece.

As our bodies approach the high noon of our physical powers, we must ask ourselves to face the Death Mother, taking the healing path and, through transformation, empowering the feminine love and strength within us that can give new birth to our vitality, spirit, and creativity. We can only invite you to take this way in life, for you must choose to seek the vial of life-giving blood.

Bibliography

Bolen, J. S. (1983). *Goddesses in everywoman: A new psychology of women.* San Francisco, CA: Harper Collins.

Bolen, J. S. (1983). *Gods in everyman: A new psychology of men's lives and loves.* San Francisco, CA: Harper Collins.

Campbell, J. (1968). *The hero with a thousand faces.* New York, NY: Princeton University Press.

Campbell, J. (2013). S. Rossi (Ed.), *Goddesses: Mysteries of the feminine divine.* Novara, CA: New World Library.

Campbell, J., & Moyers, B. (1988). *The power of myth.* New York, NY: Doubleday.

Castillejo, I. C., de. (1973). *Knowing woman.* New York, NY: Putnam.

Erikson, E. H. (1982). *The life cycle completed.* New York, NY: Norton.

Frankl, V. E. (1986). *The doctor and the soul.* New York, NY: Random House.

Fromm, E. (1964). *The heart of man.* New York, NY: Harper Collins.

Garber, M., & Vickers, N. J. (Eds.). (2002). *The Medusa reader.* New York, NY: Routledge.

Harris, B. (2002). *Sacred selfishness: A guide to living a life of substance.* Novato, CA: New World Library.

Harris, B. (2008). *Resurrecting the unicorn: Masculinity in the 21st century.* Carmel, CA: Fisher King Press.

181

Harris, B. (2014). *Becoming whole: A Jungian guide to individuation*. Asheville, NC: Spes Publications.

Harris, M., & Harris, B. (2008). *Like gold through fire: Understanding the transforming power of suffering*. Carmel, CA: Fisher King Press.

Jung, C. G. (1963). A. Jaffe (Ed.), *Memories, dreams, reflections* (R. Winston & C. Winston, Trans.). New York, NY: Pantheon, Random House.

Jung, C. G. (Ed.). (1964). *Man and his symbols*. New York, NY: Doubleday.

Kast, V. (1997). *Father-daughter, mother-son*. Rockport, MA: Elements.

Luke, H. M. (1980). The perennial feminine. *Parabola, 5*(4), 10–24.

Luke, H. M. (1988). *The voice within: Love and virtue in the age of the spirit*. New York, NY: Crossroads.

Luke, H. M. (1992). R. Baker (Ed.), *Kaleidoscope: The way of woman and other essays*. New York, NY: Parabola Books.

Megas, G. A. (Ed.). (1970). *Folktales of Greece* (H. Colaclides, Trans.). Chicago, IL: University of Chicago Press.

Metzger, D. (1992). *Writing for your life: A guide and companion to the inner world*. San Francisco, CA: Harper.

Neumann, E. (1955). *The Great Mother: An analysis of the archetype*. Princeton, NJ: Princeton University Press.

Neumann, E. (1956). *Amor and Psyche: The psychic development of the feminine*. Princeton, NJ: Princeton University Press.

Neumann, E. (1994). *The fear of the feminine and other essays on feminine psychology*. Princeton, NJ: Princeton University Press.

Qualls-Corbett, N. (2013). Redeeming the feminine: Eros and the world soul. In E. Shalit & N. S. Furlottti (Eds.), *The dream and its amplification*. Skiatook, OK: Fisher King Press.

Read, H., Fordham, M., Adler, G., & McGuire, W. (Eds.). (1954). *The collected works of C. G. Jung* (Vols. 1–20; R. F. C. Hull, Trans.). Princeton, NJ: Princeton University Press.

Shalit, E. (2002). *The complex: Path of transformation from archetype to ego.* Toronto, Canada: Inner City.

Shalit, E. (2008). *Enemy, cripple and beggar: Shadows in the hero's path.* San Francisco, CA: Fisher King Press.

Shalit, E. (2011). *The cycle of life: Themes and tales of the journey.* Carmel, CA: Fisher King Press.

Singer, J. (1998). *Modern woman in search of a soul.* York Beach, ME: Nicolas-Hays.

Ulanov, H. B. (2013). *Madness and creativity.* College Station, TX: Texas A & M University Press.

Van der Post, L. (1976). *Jung and the story of our time.* New York, NY: Viking Penguin.

Whitmont, E. C. (1969). *The symbolic quest: Basic concepts of analytical psychology.* Princeton, NJ: Princeton University Press.

Wolff, T. (1985). *Structural forms of the feminine psyche.* Zurich, Switzerland: C. G. Jung Institute.

Woodman, M. (1985). *The pregnant virgin.* Toronto, Canada: Inner City Books.

Woodman, M. (1993). *Conscious femininity.* Toronto, Canada: Inner City Books.

Woodman, M., & Sieff, D. (2009). Confronting the Death Mother: An interview with Marion Woodman. *Spring, 81,* 177–179.

Zweig, C. (Ed.). (1990). *To be a woman: The birth of the conscious feminine.* Los Angeles, CA: Tarcher.

Index

Authors' Bios

Massimilla Harris, Ph.D., is a Jungian analyst with a practice in Asheville, North Carolina for the past 25 years. She holds a doctorate in Psychology and is a graduate of the C. G. Jung Institute in Zurich, Switzerland. She is also an author, teacher, award-winning quilter, and certified Solisten Provider. Developed by Dr. Alfred A. Tomatis, Solisten is a special kind of music therapy that, along with Jungian analysis, enables Dr. Harris to help people bring mind and body together to release their full potentials.

Bud Harris, Ph.D., originally became a businessman and successfully owned his own business before returning to school to become a psychotherapist. After earning his Ph.D. in psychology and practicing as a psychotherapist and psychologist, he experienced the call to further his growth and become a Jungian analyst. He then moved to Zürich, Switzerland where he trained for over five years and graduated from the C. G. Jung Institute. He is the author of ten books, lectures widely, and practices as a Jungian analyst in Asheville, North Carolina.

For additional information about their practice and their work, visit:
www.budharris.com.

Made in the USA
Lexington, KY
02 April 2017